AMAZING!

CANADIAN NEWSPAPER STORIES

AMAZING!

CANADIAN NEWSPAPER STORIES

WRITTEN AND ILLUSTRATED BY
SUSAN BATES

VANCOUVER COMMUNITY COLLEGE

PRENTICE-HALL CANADA INC., SCARBOROUGH, ONTARIO

Canadian Cataloguing in Publication Data

Bates, Susan, 1955-
    Amazing!: Canadian newspaper stories

ISBN 0-13-026014-2

1. English language — Textbooks for second
language learners.* 2. Readers (Adult).
3. Reading (Adult education) — Problems, exercises,
etc. 4. Reading comprehension — Problems,
exercises, etc. I. Title.

PE1128.B38 1990   428.6'4   C90-093782-3

© 1991 Prentice-Hall Canada Inc., Scarborough, Ontario

Prentice-Hall, Inc., Englewood Cliffs, New Jersey
Prentice-Hall International, Inc., London
Prentice-Hall of Australia, Pty., Ltd., Sydney
Prentice-Hall of India Pvt., Ltd., New Delhi
Prentice-Hall of Japan, Inc., Tokyo
Prentice-Hall of Southeast Asia (Pte.) Ltd., Singapore
Editora Prentice-Hall do Brasil Ltda., Rio de Janeiro
Prentice-Hall Hispanoamericana, S.A., Mexico

ISBN 0-13-026014-2
Production Coordinator: *Anna Mascioli*
Production Editor: *Kelly Dickson*
Typesetting: *Anita Macklin*

1 2 3 AP 92 91 90

Printed and bound in Canada by Alger Press Limited

TABLE OF CONTENTS

*It Happened in Milestone *Crop Farming in Canada *Wheat Farmer Asks Big Question! *What Happens Next? *Surprise *Reading For Answers *Headlines *True or False *Word Families *Interview: You Work For the Newspaper *Inviting *Interview: Marriage and Wedding Customs

*Pets *It Happened in Vancouver *Debbie's Dog *Gia: An Amazing Dog! *Questions and Answers *The Eighty Commands *Prefixes *Complimenting *Discrimination *Questions and Answers

*It Happened in Toronto *What's the Story? *Roop Catches Falling Child *What Happens Next? *Catch of the Year *Reading for Answers *Headlines *Interview: You Work For the Newspaper *Opposites *You Don't Need a Dictionary! *Video Press Conference *Becoming a Canadian Citizen *Understanding the Application *Interview With a Judge

INTRODUCTION

TO THE INSTRUCTOR

Amazing! Canadian Newspaper Stories is a reading and language textbook specifically designed for mid–beginner to low–intermediate English as a Second Language students. An emphasis on developing reading skills also makes it useful for native speakers enrolled in literacy programs.

Graphically illustrated newspaper stories provide opportunities for interactive storytelling and endless listening and speaking practice as a prelude to reading stylistically authentic human-interest newspaper stories. Additional pre-reading activities feature newspaper photographs, headlines and captions, as well as Canadian facts and provincial maps highlighting various locales from across the country. A wide variety of reading skills exercises focusing on skimming, scanning, main idea, inference, and evaluation, combined with newspaper reporter role plays, paired interviews, classroom discussions, student interactions, and writing assignments expand the reading lesson into a fully integrated language learning experience.

AN INTERACTIVE APPROACH

Amazing! promotes an interactive approach to reading and language learning. Current trends in reading pedagogy and psycholinguistics suggest that comprehension is achieved through the reader's interaction with the text.[1] This necessitates the activating and building of background knowledge so that students will have a basis for understanding and prediction. Pre–reading exercises which guide students to make guesses about the content of the text orient them to a reading process in which they continue to make predictions while reading, and then read to confirm or deny these predictions. Further interaction with the text is required in the post–reading sections. The exercises focus on synthesizing information, making inferences, and relating the story to their own experience.

The book is interactive in the general sense as well. Reading cannot and should not be taught in isolation. For this reason, many of the exercises are designed so that students work in groups or with a partner, thus encouraging listening and speaking practice. Further aural/oral activities are included so that students can improve their performance in these areas. There are functional dialogues, role plays, group discussions, oral interviews, interaction activities, contact assignments, and brainstorming exercises. Increased proficiency in general language ability serves to increase reading ability and vice versa.[2] As instructors of the language, we owe it to our students to promote reading as a strategy for language acquisition.

[1] Mark A. Clarke and Sandra Silberstein, "Toward a Realization of Psycholinguistic Principles in the ESL Reading Class" in *Reading In A Second Language: Hypotheses, Organization and Practice*, eds. Mackay, Barkman, and Jordon (Rowley, Massachusetts: Newbury House Publishers Inc., 1979) pp. 48–65.

[2] Joanne Devine, "The Relationship Between General Language Competence and Second Language Reading Proficiency: Implications For Teaching" in Interactive Approaches to Second Language Reading, eds. Patricia Carrell, Joanne Devine, David Eskey, (Cambridge University Press, 1988) pp. 260–277.

CANADIAN CONTENT

If we agree that our students should be guided to improve their reading competence so that their general language performance will be enhanced, what then should our students read?

As instructors, we know that our students want to learn about Canada. Many are interested in obtaining citizenship and all want to gain insight into the culture and learn more about the country. This book provides them with much of the information they are looking for. The stories feature ordinary Canadians, and teach culture in a natural context. Provincial maps highlighting the locales of these stories are included in the pre–reading sections. Students learn basic facts about Canadian geography, and refer to their two–page map of Canada in the introduction to clearly establish the setting. Additional exercises related to citizenship and culture are featured throughout the text. They teach content and appeal to learners who want to increase their general knowledge about Canada and its people.

LEVEL

The stories range in level from mid–beginner to low–intermediate. The instructor's manual provides supplementary materials (authentic newspaper articles, simplified text and picture card masters) which allow instructors to adapt stories to the needs of their specific students.

THE CHAPTERS

The chapters are sequenced in order of difficulty with regard to the familiarity of underlying themes or concepts, complexity of the story line and length of the reading selection.

Each chapter identifies the reading process for students and is divided into seven major sections:

Getting Ready To Read

Activities in this section focus on building background knowledge and guiding students to predict what the text will be about. A discussion of the setting and key concepts related to the theme of the story familiarizes students with new vocabulary and sets the stage for reading. The particular exercises vary depending on the story being studied and include newspaper photographs, headlines, captions, key words, guided questions, cloze procedures, mapping exercises, oral interviews, and interaction activities.

Understanding the Story

This section develops a global understanding of the story by presenting it in a visual format. Students and instructor unfold the events together in an interactive storytelling session. The instructor provides only limited information and elicits the rest through the visuals.

In some chapters, there is also a picture–text matching activity which facilitates comprehension by allowing students to match segments of a text with their corresponding picture frames.

Another version of this activity is included in the "Supplementary Materials" section of the instructor's manual for each chapter. Rather than filling in numbers to represent the correct order of the text, students can actually move around text and/or picture cards until they have them sequenced correctly.

Reading the Story

Readings are presented in the form of authentic newspaper stories. The original articles have been rewritten so that with adequate preparation, beginners can understand them. The stories are stylistically authentic and represent a variety of formats one would expect to find in the newspaper.

A pre-reading question guides students to skim the article for general understanding. Line numbers are provided to allow for a discussion of fine points (pronoun referents, vocabulary items) after the initial reading.

Do You Understand the Story?

These comprehension tasks are designed to help students gain a thorough understanding of the story. They include skimming, scanning, finding the main idea, making inferences, expressing opinions, completing an outline, filling in charts, plus true/false questions, and pronoun reference exercises.

Words, Words, Words!

The vocabulary section emphasizes the importance of finding the meaning of new words through the use of context clues, and includes exercises on word forms, compound words, synonyms, and antonyms.

Language, Listening/Speaking, Reading or Writing Practice

These extension activities present information from the reading in a new way or actually extend the information by presenting new material related to the story. An example of the first activity is a newspaper–interview role play in which one student plays the part of a newspaper reporter and interviews the main character from the story.

Activities which fit into the second category include scanning newspaper advertisements, finding information in a pamphlet, reading passages about the country, writing a letter, and filling in an application form.

What About You?

This section gives students an opportunity to exchange ideas and relate the reading to their lives and experience. The exercises are conversational in nature, and often lend themselves to beginning composition. There are oral interviews, brainstorming activities, one–sided dialogues, discussion questions, and writing assignments.

THE ANSWER KEY

Answers for exercises instructors may want to use as quizzes are in the Quiz Key at the back of the instructor's manual. All other answers are in the Answer Key at the back of the student book.

THE INSTRUCTOR'S MANUAL

The manual provides clear instructions for using all exercises in the student book. In addition, it includes supplementary activities and materials. There are authentic newspaper articles, songs, and reproducible black line masters which instructors can use to make overhead transparencies, sets of eighteen simplified text and picture cards, life-size character faces for blackboard dialogue practice, and conversation spinners or cubes for group discussion purposes.

ACKNOWLEDGEMENTS

First of all, I would like to thank Pat Ferrier, managing editor from Prentice-Hall Canada, for expressing an interest in my work and offering guidance in its development.

Second, I gratefully acknowledge the editorial assistance of both Jean Ferrier and Kelly Dickson in bringing the book through the production process.

Third, I would like to thank my reviewers, Elizabeth Taborek from the Toronto Board, Continuing Education, and Ian Marquis from the Overland Learning Centre. Their comments and suggestions at each stage of development provided me with an invaluable resource for revision and refinement.

I would also like to express my sincere appreciation to the administration and faculty of King Edward Campus, Vancouver Community College for their generous support throughout the development and field testing of this textbook.

Especially, I would like to thank Dr. Patricia Groves and Norm Dooley for providing an atmosphere in which materials development projects are given a chance to flourish, Shirley Hsu, Sharon Yoneda, and Dr. Nancy Yildez for their guidance with the initial proposal, Frank Cosco for organizing a thorough field testing of every chapter, Lee Aceman, Betty-Ann Buss, Madeline Charalambous, Peter Clark, Raminder Dosanjh, June Dragman, Alex Drahotsky, Laurie Gould, Jennifer House, Dale Hunter, Raymonde Jabaji, Cheryl Jibodh, Diane Jones, Chris Joyce, Pat Kennedy, Nina Kozakiewicz, Felicia Klingenberg, Renate Lenner-Brandt, Lyn Lennig, Maeva Lightheart, Cammi MacKinlay, Donna McGee, Cameron McNamee, Angela McWhirter, Petra Makarewicz, Alison Norman, Robert Peck, Sarah Plamenig, Grant Richards, Herbert Saltzman, Anne Sander, Tanis Sawkins, Candice Slattery, Lynda Stewart, Ed Soltis, Judy Taylor, Fraser Thorburn, Maggie Trebble, Mary Waddington, Mike Webb, Jack Whalen, and Susan Yee-MacMillan for their feedback and encouragement, Ida Barazzuol, Chris Clark, Hughie Jones, Doris Kiernan and Dan Rieb for their helpful suggestions, Linda Nightingale and Joan Cawsey for their newspaper role-play activity, Stan, Peggy, and Barbara Wood for background information pertaining to Chapter 6, Carla Pitton for her drawings of Canadian crops, Lauchlin McKenzie for his photographic expertise, Irene Strong for her review of the instructor's manual, and Khatun Siddiqi for a final analysis of the text with regard to the interactive approach to reading and its practical applications.

Finally, I would like to thank my close friends and family for their inspiration and support.

TO THE STUDENT

This is a book about Canada and Canadians. Each of the twelve chapters includes an interesting newspaper story and exercises to help you with your English. The first chapter is the easiest. As you read through the book, the stories and exercises get more and more difficult. There is an answer key at the back of the book so you can check the exercises after you finish them.

At the beginning of most chapters, you will find out where the story happens and answer questions about Canadian geography. Your map of Canada will help you do this. Before you start reading, turn the page and study the map. Then, answer these questions:

1. What are the names of the ten provinces?

    _____   _____

    _____   _____

    _____   _____

    _____   _____

    _____   _____

2. What are the names of the two territories?

    _____   _____

3. Which ocean is east of Canada?

    _____

4. Which ocean is west of Canada?

    _____

5. What is the capital of Canada?

    _____

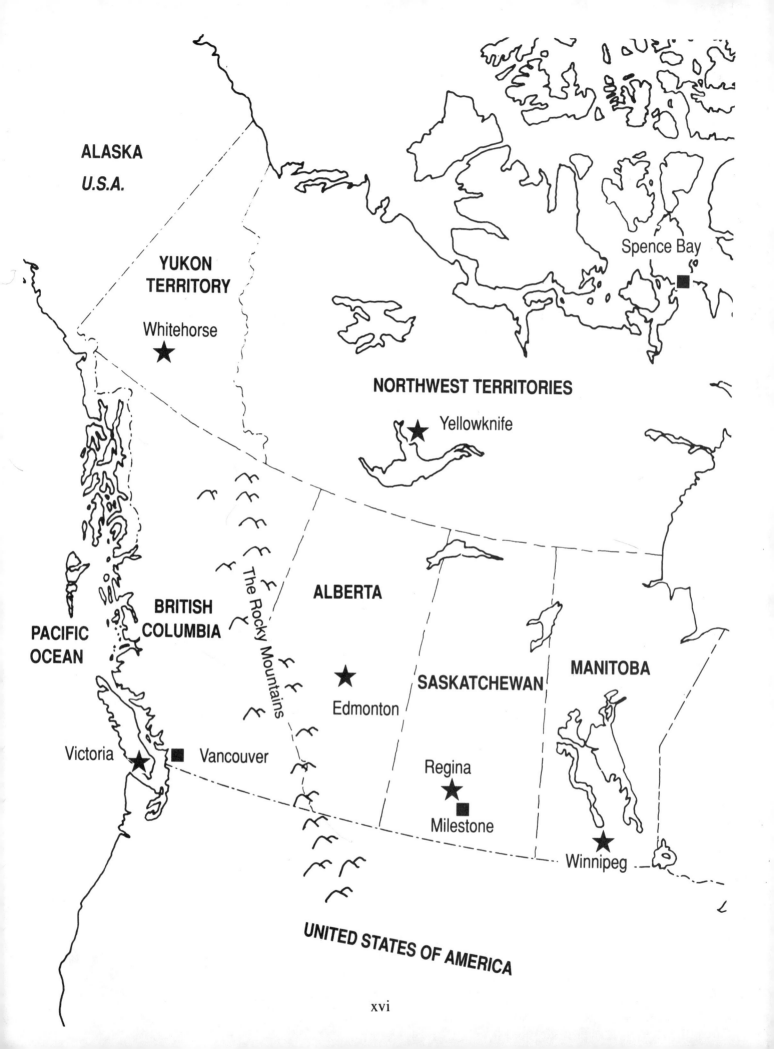

ALASKA

U.S.A.

YUKON
TERRITORY

Whitehorse ★

Spence Bay ■

NORTHWEST TERRITORIES

★ Yellowknife

PACIFIC
OCEAN

BRITISH
COLUMBIA

The Rocky Mountains

ALBERTA

★
Edmonton

SASKATCHEWAN

MANITOBA

Victoria ★ ■ Vancouver

Regina
★

Milestone ■

★
Winnipeg

UNITED STATES OF AMERICA

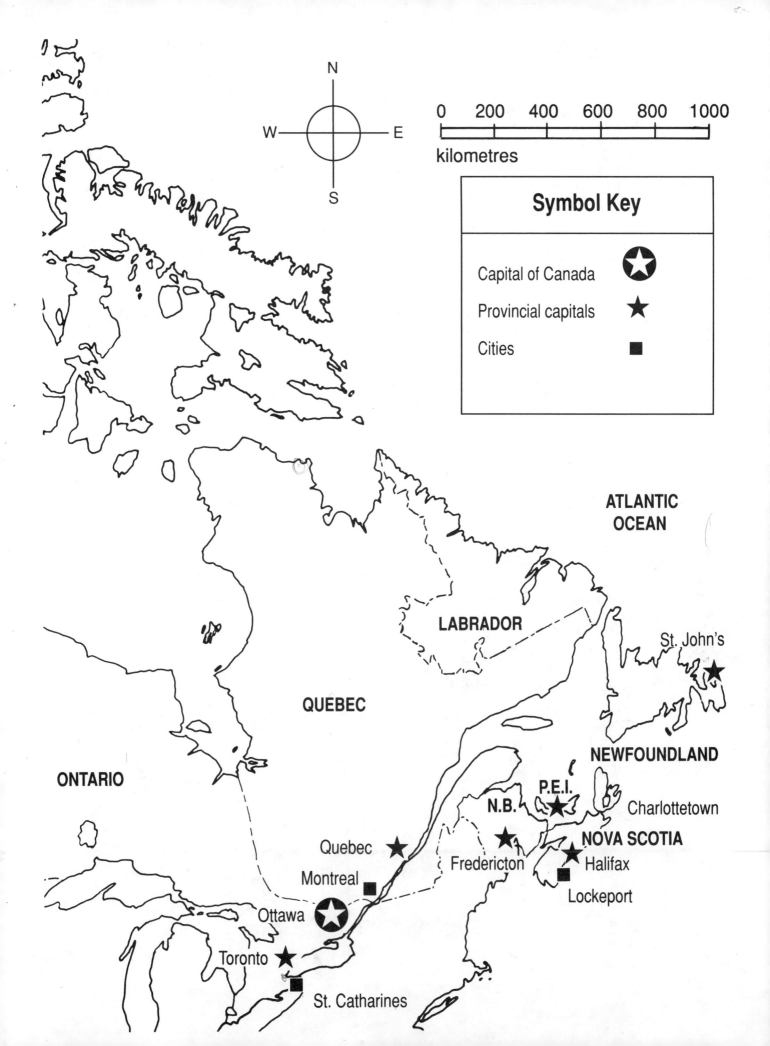

N
W   E
S

0   200   400   600   800   1000
kilometres

Symbol Key

Capital of Canada   ✪

Provincial capitals   ★

Cities   ■

ATLANTIC OCEAN

LABRADOR

St. John's

QUEBEC

NEWFOUNDLAND

ONTARIO

P.E.I.

N.B.   Charlottetown

NOVA SCOTIA

Quebec

Fredericton   Halifax

Montreal

Lockeport

Ottawa

Toronto

St. Catharines

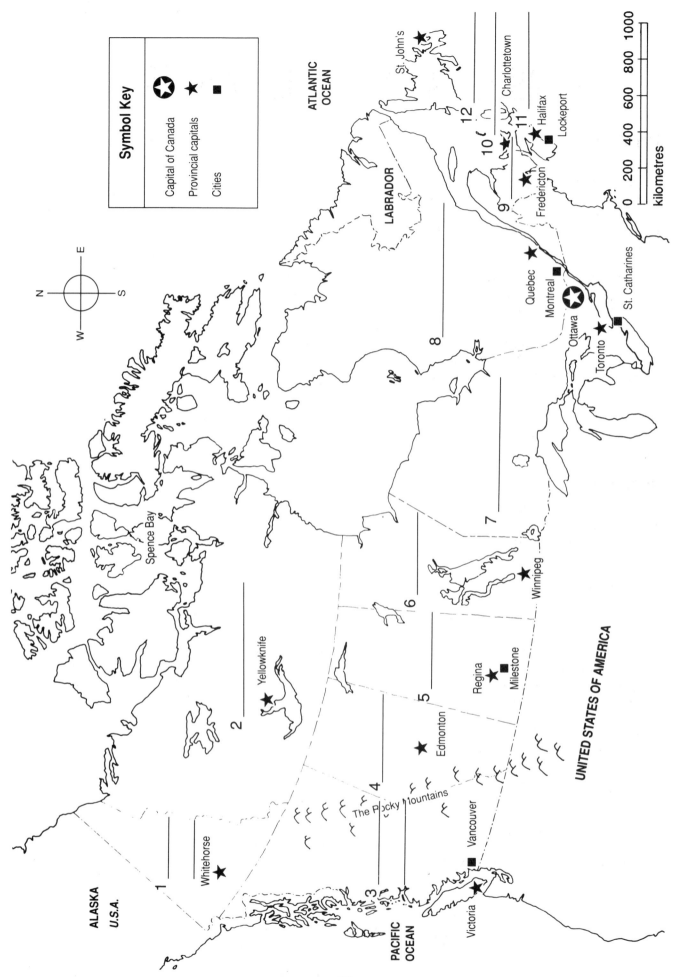

PHOTO AND ARTICLE CREDITS

Photos

Articles

O CANADA

With the Class

Sing Canada's National Anthem.

O CANADA

O Canada! Our home and native land

True patriot love in all thy sons' command.

With glowing hearts we see thee rise

The true north strong and free,

From far and wide, O Canada,

We stand on guard for thee.

God keep our land glorious and free,

O Canada, we stand on guard for thee.

O Canada, we stand on guard for thee.

Sing your country's national anthem to the class.

CHAPTER 1

IT HAPPENED IN MILESTONE

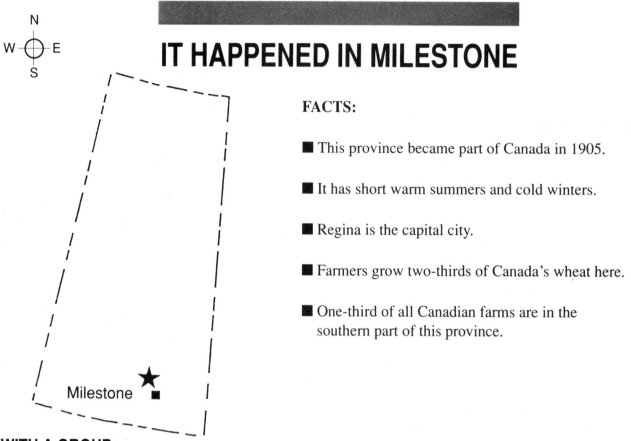

FACTS:

■ This province became part of Canada in 1905.

■ It has short warm summers and cold winters.

■ Regina is the capital city.

■ Farmers grow two-thirds of Canada's wheat here.

■ One-third of all Canadian farms are in the southern part of this province.

WITH A GROUP

Find Milestone on your map of Canada. Answer these questions:

1. Which province is Milestone in?

_____

2. What is the capital of this province? Write it on the map.

_____

3. Is Milestone in eastern or western Canada?

_____

4. What do farmers grow in this part of the country?

_____

CROP FARMING IN CANADA

WITH A PARTNER

Here are some of Canada's important crops.
Draw a line from the name of the crop to its picture.

1. wheat

2. apples

3. pears

4. corn

5. cherries

6. plums

7. grapes

8. potatoes

9. strawberries

10. peaches

11. blueberries

12. maple syrup

Read the chart below. What do farmers grow in each part of the country?

CROP FARMING IN CANADA

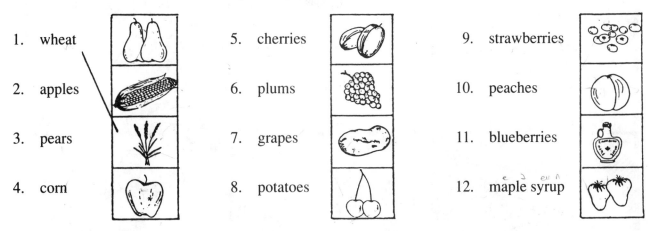

B.C. (Okanagan)	
Prairies	
Southern Ontario	
Southern Quebec	
Maritimes	

CLASS DISCUSSION

1. What do you know about farmers?
2. What crops do farmers grow in your country?

WHEAT FARMER ASKS BIG QUESTION!

WITH THE INSTRUCTOR Answer questions about the pictures and tell the story together.

Retell the story with a partner.

* Instructor's Manual
Simplified Text and Picture Card Masters

WHAT HAPPENS NEXT?

WITH A PARTNER

Write a number in each box. Look at the picture story for help. Number one is done for you.

Chuck loved Cecile very much and wanted to marry her. 3	The proposal was one and a half kilometres long and said, "Will you marry me Cecile? Love Chuck." 7	Later, Chuck had an idea. 4
Chuck cut a marriage proposal for Cecile in his best wheat field. He finished it at 1:45 P.M. 6	Chuck lives in Milestone, Saskatchewan. He is a wheat farmer. 1	At 9:00 A.M., he got on his tractor, and started to cut some wheat. 5
Cecile is his girlfriend. She works at Sun Life, a company in Regina. 2	When she looked down and saw the proposal, she smiled and answered "Yes!" 9	Later that afternoon, Chuck rented a plane and flew Cecile over the wheat field. 8

* Instructor's Manual
Text and Picture Card Masters

What is surprising about this story?

July 17

SURPRISE

MILESTONE, SASKATCHEWAN —
Chuck, a thirty-one-year-old wheat farmer
from Milestone, proposed marriage in a
very surprising way yesterday, He cut the
proposal in his wheat field.   5

Chuck got on his tractor at nine o'clock
in the morning and finished four hours and
forty-five minutes later. The proposal was
one and a half kilometres long and said,   10
"Will you marry me Cecile? Love Chuck."

Later that afternoon, he rented a plane
and flew his girlfriend over the wheat field.
When she looked down and saw the words,
she smiled and answered, "Yes!"   15
Cecile, an office worker from Regina,
said she was very happy about the
proposal.

---

*Instructor's Manual
Original Newspaper Article

DO YOU UNDERSTAND THE STORY?

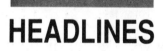

READING FOR ANSWERS

How fast can you find the answers in the story?

1. How old is Chuck?

   _____ - _____ years old.

2. When did he propose to Cecile?

   _____

3. How long did he work in his wheat field?

   _____ _____ _____ _____ - _____ _____

4. How long was the proposal?

   _____ _____ _____ - _____ _____

5. When did Chuck rent the plane?

   _____ - _____ _____

HEADLINES

WITH A GROUP

Write your own headlines for the newspaper story. Use the words in each box.

1. | A FINDS WIFE FARMER |

   _____

2. | FARMER WHEAT MARRIAGE PROPOSES |

   _____

3. | PROPOSAL WRITES FIELD FARMER IN |

   _____

4. | ME ? YOU WILL MARRY |

   _____

Which headline do you like best? Why?

DO YOU UNDERSTAND THE STORY?

TRUE OR FALSE?

WITH A PARTNER

Read each sentence and write T (true) or F (false) on the line.
Write a sentence to explain your answer.

**1. Chuck is an intelligent man. ___F___

_____

*2. Chuck and Cecile live in the same city. ___F___

_____

3. It took Chuck all day to cut the proposal. ___F___

_____

4. Cecile helped Chuck cut the proposal. ___F___

_____

5. Chuck wrote, "I will marry you Cecile." in his wheat field. ___F___

_____

*6. All Canadian farmers propose like Chuck did. ___F___

_____

7. Chuck paid money to fly the plane. ___T___

_____

*8. Cecile liked Chuck's idea. ___T___

_____

8

WORD FAMILIES

WITH A PARTNER

Fill in the chart with words from the story and then complete the sentences below.

	VERB	NOUN
1	work	worker
2	marry	married
3		smile
4	proposed	proposed

1. Cecile is an office _____ worker _____.

   Chuck _____ work _____ on a farm.

2. Chuck wrote a _____ marry _____ proposal in his wheat field.

   Chuck wanted to _____ Cecile.

3. Cecile _____ smile _____ when she saw the proposal.

   She had a big _____ on her face.

4. Chuck _____ in a plane.

   Cecile said, "Yes!" to Chuck's _____.

INTERVIEW CHUCK: You work for the newspaper.

WITH A PARTNER

1. Write the missing question words and then practice the interview.
2. Cover the answers and practice the interview again.
3. Cover the questions and practice again.

1. _What_ is your job?

*I am a **wheat farmer**.*

2. _Where_ do you live?

*I live in **Milestone, Saskatchewan**.*

3. _How old_ are you?

*I am **thirty-one years old**.*

4. _Who_ is your girlfriend?

***Cecile** is my girlfriend.*

5. _Where_ does she work?

*She works **at Sun Life**.*

6. _What kind_ of work does she do?

*She is an **office worker**.*

7. _Who much_ do you love Cecile?

*I love her **very much**.*

8. _What_ idea did you have? _What kind of_

I wanted to cut a marriage proposal for Cecile in my best wheat field.

LANGUAGE PRACTICE

Change roles.

9. _____Who_____ did you cut the
(why)
wheat?

*I cut the wheat **with my tractor**.*

10. ___How___ ___long___
did it take you to cut the
proposal?

*It took me **four hours and forty–five minutes**.*

11. ___Why___ did you cut the
best wheat?

*I cut the best wheat **because I wanted the proposal to look good**.*

12. ___How___ ___long___
was the question?

*It was **one and a half kilometres long**.*

13. ___Why___ did you rent
the plane?

I wanted to fly Cecile over the proposal.

14. ___What___ did Cecile say?

*She said, "**Yes!!!!**"*

INVITING

WITH A PARTNER

Practice the conversation.

> **CHUCK:** Hi Cecile. How are you today?
> **CECILE:** Not bad. How about you?
> **CHUCK:** Pretty good. Cecile, I was thinking, uh, **would you like to** go on a plane ride this afternoon?
> **CECILE:** A plane ride — *what a great idea!* When do you want to go?
> **CHUCK:** How about I pick you up around three.
> **CECILE** *Sure.* I'll see you then.

Practice the conversation again. Use different words for "inviting" and "saying yes."

Inviting	**Saying Yes**
Do you want to...	*I'd like that.*
Do you have time to...	*I'd love to.*
How would you like to...	*(That) sounds great!*
How about _____ ing...	*(That) sounds like fun!*

Invite your partner to...

GO TO THE LIBRARY	GO TO A RESTAURANT	GO FOR A WALK

> **YOU:** Hi _____ , How's it going?
> **PARTNER:** Fine, and you?
> **YOU:** Great! _____ , I was wondering, uh, **do you have time to** GO TO THE LIBRARY with me after school?
> **PARTNER:** The library — *sure,* I have some work to do. What time do you want to go?
> **YOU:** How does four o'clock sound?
> **PARTNER:** *Sounds good to me.*

Close your book and invite your friend to a party!

* Instructor's Manual
Blackboard Dialogue Activity

INTERVIEW: Marriage and Wedding Customs

WITH A PARTNER

Ask questions and write the answers. Be ready to tell the class about wedding customs in your partner's country.

1. Where are you from?

_____

2. At what age do people usually get married in your country?

_____

3. How do they propose?

_____

4. What do they wear to the wedding?

_____

5. Does the couple have a party (reception) after the wedding?

_____

6. Do friends buy gifts? What kind?

_____

7. Who pays for the wedding?

_____

8. Does the couple go on a honeymoon? For how long?

_____

9. Does the couple live alone or with the parents?

_____

10. What do you know about marriage and wedding customs in Canada?

_____

CHAPTER 2

GETTING READY TO READ

PETS

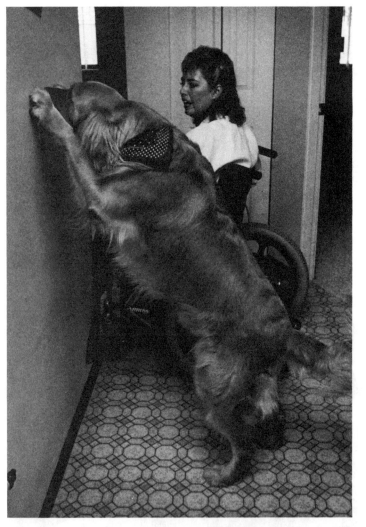

WITH A GROUP

Answer the questions.

1. What are pets?

2. Write four different kinds of pets.

   _____

   _____

   _____

   _____

3. Why do people have pets?

4. What kinds of pets do people have in your country?

5. Did you ever have a pet? Tell about it.

6. What can pets do for people with disabilities?

This is a story about a disabled woman named Debbie and her pet dog, Gia. Write four questions you have about the story.

1. _____ ?

2. _____ ?

3. _____ ?

4. _____ ?

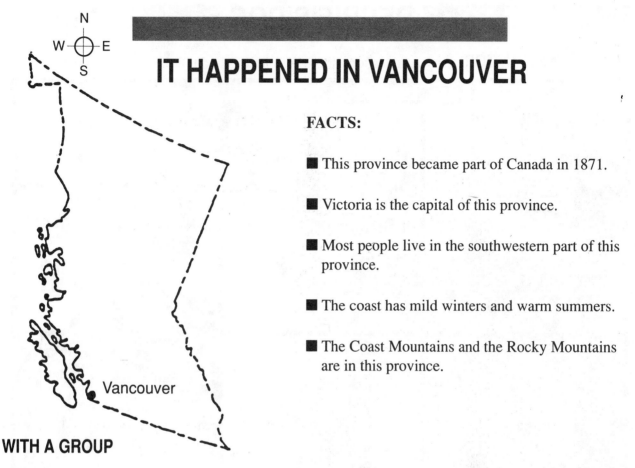

IT HAPPENED IN VANCOUVER

FACTS:

■ This province became part of Canada in 1871.

■ Victoria is the capital of this province.

■ Most people live in the southwestern part of this province.

■ The coast has mild winters and warm summers.

■ The Coast Mountains and the Rocky Mountains are in this province.

WITH A GROUP

Find Vancouver on your map of Canada. Answer these questions:

1. Which province is Vancouver in? Write it on the map.

   _____

2. Is Vancouver in eastern or western Canada?

   _____

3. What do you know about Vancouver?

   _____

4. Why is Vancouver a good place for disabled people to live?

   _____

DEBBIE'S DOG

WITH THE INSTRUCTOR Answer questions about the pictures and tell the story together.

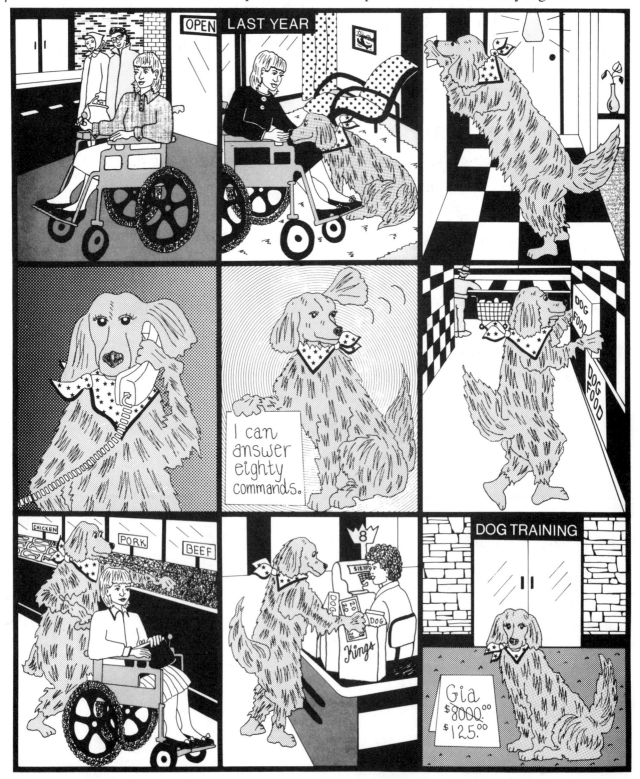

Retell the story with a partner.

* Instructor's Manual
Simplified Text and Picture Card Masters

What is amazing about Debbie's dog?

GIA: AN AMAZING DOG!

VANCOUVER, B.C. — Three years ago, Debbie McCann broke her neck in a car accident, and now she can't move her arms or legs very much. She is a disabled person and gets around in a wheelchair.

Last year, she got a dog to help her with the many things she cannot do. Gia can turn on the lights and answer the phone. In fact, he can answer eighty different commands.

When they go shopping, he picks items off the shelves, puts them in the shopping cart, pushes Debbie's wheelchair, and then, he pays the cashier!

Debbie got the dog from a nonprofit organization near Vancouver. It costs them $8000.00 to train dogs for people with disabilities. Debbie paid $125.00 and the organization paid the rest. They are a nonprofit organization: they don't want to make money; they just want to help people.

What amazing things can other animals do?

*Instructor's Manual
Original Newspaper Article*

DO YOU UNDERSTAND THE STORY?

QUESTIONS AND ANSWERS

WITH A GROUP

Talk about each question and write a group answer. The answers are not always in the story.*

1. Why is Debbie in a wheelchair?

   _____

2. Why did she get a dog?

   _____

*3. How did Gia learn to answer eighty commands?

   _____

*4. How much did the organization pay for the dog?

   _____

**5. Where do you think they got this money?

   _____

**6. Do you think it is a good idea to train dogs for disabled people? Why or why not?

   _____

CLASS DISCUSSION

1. What other nonprofit organizations do you know about?
2. Which nonprofit organizations help new Canadians?
3. How do they help them?
4. What are the names, addresses, and phone numbers of two of these organizations?

1. Name: _____ 2. Name: _____

   Address: _____   Address: _____

   _____   _____

   Phone Number: _____   Phone Number: _____

THE EIGHTY COMMANDS

WITH A GROUP

List the six commands Gia answers in the story.

1. *Turn on the lights.*
2. _____
3. _____
4. _____
5. _____
6. _____

What do you think the other seventy–four are? Write as many commands as you can think of. You have ten minutes.

_____

_____

_____

_____

_____

_____

_____

_____

_____

_____

_____

_____

Write your commands on the blackboard.

WORDS, WORDS, WORDS!

PREFIXES

Prefixes come at the beginning of words.
Find two words in the story with prefixes meaning "no" or "not." Write them here:

a) _____ b) _____

There are many other words with the prefixes "dis" and "non." Write the correct prefix in front of each of these words.

c) _____*d*_____ likes   d) _____*d*_____ abilities

e) _____*n*_____ returnable   f) _____*n*_____ profit

g) _____*n*_____ fat   h) _____*d*_____ pleased

i) _____*d*_____ interested   j) __*not*__ stop

WITH A PARTNER

Use one of these words in each of the sentences below.

1. _____ foods are good for you.

2. These bottles are _____.

3. She _____ winter because it is so cold.

4. He is _____ because his rent is $50.00 more this month.

5. There are many people with _____ living in Canada.

6. She is _____ in working because she wants to study English full–time.

7. There is a _____ plane leaving for Toronto at 4:00 P.M.

8. He works at a _____ organization.

COMPLIMENTING

WITH A PARTNER

Complete the conversation and practice it.

CASHIER: *I love your dog!*

DEBBIE: _____ .

CASHIER: Where did you get him?

DEBBIE: _____ .

CASHIER: You were lucky. How much did you pay?

DEBBIE: _____ .

CASHIER: Is that all? *He's such a helpful and friendly pet.*

DEBBIE: _____ .

CASHIER: What kind of dog is he anyway?

DEBBIE: _____ .

CASHIER: A golden retriever! They are wonderful dogs.

Make up a new conversation. Have the cashier compliment Debbie on her blouse.
You can use these expressions:

Giving Compliments	Accepting Compliments
That's a nice...	Thanks for the compliment.
I (really) like your...	How nice of you to say so.
What a beautiful/interesting...	I'm glad you like it/them/him/her.
You have a lovely...	That's nice to hear.

WITH A GROUP

Compliment each other about clothes, haircuts, and jewelry. Use the expressions above to give and accept compliments.

EXTRA   Compliment the instructor!

*Instructor's Manual
Blackboard Dialogue Activity

DISCRIMINATION

Read this newspaper article. If you do not understand a word, try to guess the meaning.

WOMAN TOLD TO GET OUT

LONDON, ONTARIO — Debbie Mayne, a 37–year–old blind woman, went into a restaurant and sat down with her guide dog. After the waiter
5 brought her coffee, the restaurant owner came in and told Debbie and her dog to get out.

Debbie said that was discrimination. She told the owner it
10 was against the law to make her leave. Her dog was quiet and was not disturbing anyone in the restaurant. Alex, the restaurant owner said, "This is my place, I make the laws...and you can take your laws with you." 15

Debbie was angry about what happened so she brought Alex to court. The judge made Alex pay $300.00 for discriminating against a blind person. Alex said "I am very 20 sorry. Debbie can come into my restaurant anytime she wants."

Match the new words with their meanings.

discrimination _____   1. person who cannot see

blind _____   2. restaurant is his or hers

guide dog _____   3. rule made by the government

restaurant owner _____   4. person who decides if you are right or wrong

law _____   5. make a lot of noise

against the law _____   6. place a judge works

disturb _____   7. do something wrong or illegal

court _____   8. dislike someone because they are different

judge _____   9. dog that helps a blind person

Read the article to answer the questions on the next page.
Tell about a time **you** or **someone you know** was discriminated against.

DO YOU UNDERSTAND?

QUESTIONS AND ANSWERS

WITH A PARTNER

One person asks the questions and the other answers. Then, change roles.

1. How old is Debbie?
   _____

2. What kind of disability does she have?
   _____

3. What kind of pet does she have?
   _____

4. How does her pet help her?
   _____

5. Where did she go?
   _____

6. What did the waiter bring for her?
   _____

7. Who came in?
   _____

8. What did he tell Debbie and her dog to do?
   _____

9. What did Debbie say?
   _____

10. Was her dog noisy in the restaurant?
    _____

11. What did Alex say about the law?
    _____

12. How did Debbie feel about what happened in the restaurant?
    _____

13. What did she do?
    _____

14. What did the judge make Alex do?
    _____

15. What did Alex say?
    _____

**16. Do you think Debbie will go to that restaurant again?
    _____

CHAPTER 3

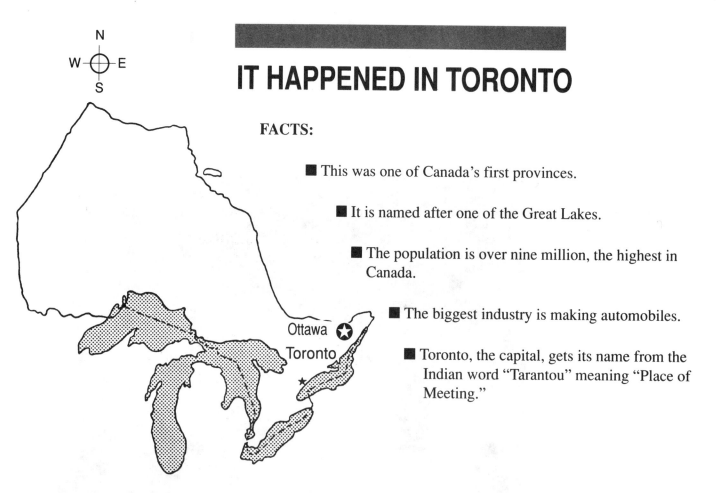

IT HAPPENED IN TORONTO

FACTS:

- ■ This was one of Canada's first provinces.

- ■ It is named after one of the Great Lakes.

- ■ The population is over nine million, the highest in Canada.

- ■ The biggest industry is making automobiles.

- ■ Toronto, the capital, gets its name from the Indian word "Tarantou" meaning "Place of Meeting."

WITH A GROUP

Find Toronto on your map of Canada. Answer these questions:

1. Which province is Toronto in? Write it on the map.

_____

2. What is the capital of this province?

_____

3. What other capital is in this province?

_____

4. What do you know about Toronto?

_____

WHAT'S THE STORY?

WITH A GROUP

Talk about the picture. Label it with these key words.

Roop Sandhu   **balcony**   **highrise apartment building**   **catch**

1. _____

2. _____

3. _____

What do you think this newspaper story is about?

ROOP CATCHES FALLING CHILD

WITH THE INSTRUCTOR Answer questions about the pictures and tell the story together.

Retell the story with a partner.

* Instructor's Manual
Simplified Text and Picture Card Masters

WHAT HAPPENS NEXT?

WITH A PARTNER

Write a number in each box. Look at the picture story for help. Number one is done for you.

Eric **hung onto** the edge for two minutes and screamed, "Daddy, Daddy!" but his father didn't hear him. _____	After a while, Eric and his father **fell asleep.** _____	He pushed a chair onto the balcony and **climbed up.** _____
Sandhu **threw aside** his tools, ran one hundred metres, and **jumped over** a 1.2 metre fence. _____	The Minhas family live on the sixth floor of a highrise apartment building near Toronto. One day Mr. Minhas was watching T.V. with his son, Eric. Mrs. Minhas was going to work. __1__	Then, he **held out** his arms and caught the falling boy. _____
Later, Eric **woke up** because he heard some children playing outside. _____	He **stood on** the railing and **looked down** to see the children. Then he slipped and **fell over** the edge. _____	Roop Sandhu heard the scream while he was **working on** his car. He **looked up** and saw the boy **hanging from** the balcony. _____

*Instructor's Manual
Text Card and Picture Masters

Why is this newspaper story called, "Catch of the Year"?
What new information can you find in the newspaper story?

March 30

CATCH OF THE YEAR

Roop Sandhu

TORONTO, ONTARIO — Roop Sandhu made the catch of the year on the weekend.

5 Sandhu saw a young child hanging from a sixth-floor apartment balcony, ran one 10 hundred metres, jumped over a 1.2 metre fence, and held out his arms to catch the falling child.

Eric Minhas, only three years old, knocked Sandhu down when 15 he fell. The boy is in the hospital but doctors say he'll be OK.

The Minhas family live in a highrise apartment building just outside Toronto. On the day of the 20 accident, Mrs. Minhas was at work and Eric was at home with his father. They both fell asleep while they were watching TV.

Eric woke up a little later when he heard children playing outside. He pushed a chair onto the balcony, 25 and climbed up to see them. When he looked down, he accidentally slipped and fell over the edge. He hung on for a couple of minutes and screamed for his father, but his 30 father didn't hear him.

Sandhu, a mechanic, was fixing his car when he heard the scream. He looked up and saw Eric hanging from the balcony. He quickly threw 35 aside his tools, and started running, arms out.

"He saved my son's life," said the boy's mother. "I don't know how to thank him." 40

"I didn't want the boy to be hurt," said Sandhu, who emigrated from India two and a half years ago.

*Instructor's Manual
Original Newspaper Article

READING FOR ANSWERS

How fast can you find the answers in the story?

1. What floor does the Minhas family live on?

    They live on the _____ floor _____ .

2. How far did Roop run?

    He ran _____ _____ _____ .

3. How high was the fence.

    It was _____ _____ high.

4. How old is Eric?

    He is _____ _____ _____ .

5. How long did Eric hang on to the balcony?

    He hung on for _____ _____ _____ _____ .

6. When did Sandhu come to Canada?

    He came to Canada _____ _____ _____ _____ years ago.

HEADLINES

WITH A GROUP

A headline tells the story in a few words. Check ☑ the headlines that tell the story.

1. ❑ FATHER FALLS ASLEEP

2. ❑ SANDHU SAVES BOY

3. ❑ NEW IMMIGRANT SAVES A LIFE

4. ❑ ROOP FIXES CAR

5. ❑ GOOD CATCH ROOP!

6. ❑ THE FLYING BOY

Write your own headline for the story. _____

INTERVIEW: You work for the newspaper

WORK IN GROUPS OF THREE

1. Make questions to ask Roop Sandhu. Use the pictures and the key words to help you.
2. Have the interview. One person is the reporter. One person is Roop, and one person checks the answer key.

1. Where / Minhas family live?

    _____

2. Where / mother go?

    _____

3. What / father and son do?

    _____

4. What happened / a while?

    _____

5. Why / Eric wake up?

    _____

6. What / he push onto / balcony?

    _____

DO YOU UNDERSTAND THE STORY?

Change roles.

7. How / he get / the edge of the balcony?

   _____

8. What / then?

   _____

9. How long / he hold on?

   _____

10. What / he scream?

   _____

11. Where / you at the time?

   _____

12. What / you do?

   _____

13. Why / you catch the boy?

   _____

14. How / you feel?

   _____

WORDS, WORDS, WORDS!

OPPOSITES

WITH A PARTNER

Find the words in the story that are opposite to these words. Write them on the lines.

1. lowrise _____
2. awake _____
3. working _____
4. inside _____
5. pulled _____
6. whisper _____
7. old _____
8. slowly _____
9. caught _____
10. immigrated _____

YOU DON'T NEED A DICTIONARY!

WITH A PARTNER

Look back at the story to make sure you understand the meaning of these words. Then, write them in the correct spaces in the paragraph below.

fence	scream	fixing	save	climbed	quickly
tools	edge	metres	hurt	accidentally	knocked

    Eric was playing on the balcony outside his apartment. He _____ [1] onto the

railing and screamed when he _____ [2] fell over the _____ [3].

Luckily, Eric wasn't badly _____ [4] because Roop heard Eric's

_____ [5] while he was _____ [6] his car. He threw aside his

_____ [7], ran one hundred _____ [8], and jumped over a 1.2-metre

_____ [9] to _____ [10] the boy.

    Because Eric was falling so _____ [11], he _____ [12] Sandhu down

as he fell to the ground.

LANGUAGE PRACTICE

VIDEO PRESS CONFERENCE

WITH THE CLASS

Roop, Eric, Mr. and Mrs. Minhas are here today for a press conference. You are the reporters and can ask questions. Write one question to ask each person.

Roop: _____ ?

Eric: _____ ?

Mr. Minhas: _____ ?

Mrs. Minhas: _____ ?

Ask four students to act as these people from the story. All other students are reporters, and go up one at a time to ask questions. Videotape the conference.

CLASS DISCUSSION

1. Do you know another story like this one? Tell the class.
2. Were you or your children ever in a dangerous situation? Tell what happened.
3. Did you ever help someone or save someone's life? Tell what happened.

BECOMING A CANADIAN CITIZEN

WITH A PARTNER

Roop has been in Canada for two and a half years. Soon he can apply for citizenship. Scan the pamphlet about Canadian citizenship to answer these questions.

1. How long do you have to live in Canada to become a citizen?

   _____

2. Can you be a citizen of two countries?

   _____

3. What do you have to know to become a citizen?

   _____

4. How do you prepare for the interview with the judge?

   _____

5. What papers do you need to apply for citizenship?

   _____

WHY BECOME A CITIZEN?

— you can vote
— you can apply for any job
— you can run for political office (You can be Prime Minister!)
— you have the freedom to travel in and out of the country
— you can be a citizen of more than one country
— you can keep your own culture

WHO CAN BECOME A CITIZEN?

— you have to be a permanent resident (landed immigrant) and have lived in Canada for three out of the last four years
— you have to know English or French
— you have to know about Canadian history, geography, and government
— you have to have a birth certificate or passport, immigration visa, citizenship photos, two other pieces of I.D., and, if applicable, a marriage certificate and/or a change of name certificate

HOW TO BECOME A CITIZEN

— pick up an application at a Secretary of State government office
— complete the application
— sign the application in front of a court officer and show your documents
— prepare for the interview by taking a citizenship class, or by reading the pamphlets from the citizenship office
— go to the interview with the judge
— go to the citizenship ceremony

Read the information more carefully and write questions to ask your partner.

UNDERSTANDING THE APPLICATION

WITH A GROUP

Read the application* and write any words you don't understand on the blackboard. Discuss these words with the class.

Surname						Given name (s)	

1. Mr. ❑   Miss ❑
   Mrs. ❑   Ms. ❑

Place and Country of Birth	Birthdate	Sex	Height	Colour of Eyes
	Y | M | D	F | M		
			cm	

Present Address in Full

Telephone Number (include area code)
Residence   Business
(   )   (   )

Occupation

Nationality

2. Marital Status
Single ❑   Married ❑   Widow(er) ❑
Divorced ❑   Separated ❑

Place and Country of Marriage(s) Date (s)
Y \| M \| D

If ever married, give particulars of spouse. If married more than once, give details of each marriage.

Surname (at birth)   **Given name(s)**

Is your spouse a citizen of this country   No ❑   By Naturalization ❑
                                                                 or
                                                                 Yes ❑   By Birth ❑

Spouse's Place and Country of Birth   **Birthdate**
                                                                                     Y \| M \| D

3. Your Name on Entry to this Country   **Entry date**
                                                                                     Y \| M \| D

Place of Entry   **Name and Type of Transport**   **Entry date**
                                                                                     Y \| M \| D

*This is a sample application. You can get a real one at your local Citizenship Court.

WHAT ABOUT YOU?

INTERVIEW WITH A JUDGE

The following is an example of an interview with a citizenship judge. The questions are only a sample of what the judge may ask to find out if you have a good knowledge of Canada and know about your rights and responsibilities as a Canadian citizen. You can find out everything you need to know for your interview by reading "A Look at Canada" and "The Canadian Citizen." These are available at your local Citizenship Court. You can also obtain them by writing to:

> Registrar of Canadian Citizenship
> Citizenship Registration and Promotion Branch
> Ottawa, Ontario
> K1A 0M5

WITH A PARTNER

Practice the interview several times.
Sometimes, be the judge and sometimes, be the applicant.

JUDGE: Good morning. How are you today?

APPLICANT: _____

JUDGE: I understand you want to be a Canadian citizen?

APPLICANT: _____

JUDGE: Good, so can you tell me what the capital of Canada is?

APPLICANT: _____

JUDGE: Uh–huh, and who is the Prime Minister of Canada?

APPLICANT: _____

JUDGE: Yes, and do you know who Canada's first Prime Minister was?

APPLICANT: _____

WHAT ABOUT YOU?

JUDGE: Now tell me, how many provinces and territories are there in Canada?

APPLICANT: _____

JUDGE: And do you know what the three levels of government are?

APPLICANT: _____

JUDGE: Yes, and who is the Premier of this province?

APPLICANT: _____

JUDGE: Mm–hmm, and what can you tell me about your rights as a Canadian citizen?

APPLICANT: _____

JUDGE: And how about your responsibilities—what do you know about your responsibilities as a Canadian citizen?

APPLICANT: _____

JUDGE: Good, now why do we have a holiday on July 1st?

APPLICANT: _____

JUDGE: Yes, and tell me what is Canada's population?

APPLICANT: _____

JUDGE: You've answered all my questions and you seem to know a lot about Canada. I hope that both you and our country can gain much from each other.

APPLICANT: _____

PLEASE NOTE:
These questions are only examples of what the citizenship judge may ask you. She/he will probably ask more questions and some may be about different subjects. It is very important that you study all the information in "The Canadian Citizen" and "A Look at Canada."*

*This exercise was written in collaboration with the Deputy Registrar of Canadian Citizenship.

CHAPTER 4

WORLD TRAVEL

WITH A GROUP

When you travel from one place to another place, you can travel in many different ways.
Write them here.

by plane _____   _____

_____   _____   _____

_____   _____   _____

INTERVIEW YOUR PARTNER — ASK ABOUT A PLACE SHE/HE TRAVELLED

1. Where did you travel? Show me on the world map (page 53).

   _____

2. When did you travel?

   _____

3. How did you travel?

   _____

4. Why did you travel?

   _____

5. Who(m) did you travel with?

   _____

6. How long did you stay?

   _____

7. What interesting things did you see?

   _____

8. Tell about an interesting thing that happened.

   _____

9. Did you meet anyone you liked? Tell about this person.

   _____

10. Would you like to go back? Why or why not?

   _____

WHAT'S THE STORY?

LOVERS UNITED

News Services
ST. CATHARINES, Ont.

Olga from Czechoslovakia and Vladimir
from the U.S.S.R. are back together.

WITH A GROUP?

What do you think this newspaper story is about?

_____

_____

_____

_____

_____

Write four questions you have about the story.

1. _____ ?

2. _____ ?

3. _____ ?

4. _____ ?

FINALLY!

WITH THE INSTRUCTOR Answer questions about the pictures and tell the story together.

Retell the story with a partner.

* Instructor's Manual
Simplified Text and Picture Card Masters

What year did Olga and Vladimir fall in love?

March 29

LOVERS UNITED

ST. CATHARINES, ONTARIO — Finally, thirty-one years after they first met, Olga and Vladimir are getting married.

5   They met in the Soviet Union when they were both twenty years old. Olga was travelling around the country with a group of students from her hometown in

10 Czechoslovakia. Vladimir was a young Russian sailor. "I remember when I first saw him," said Olga, "He was so tanned and so handsome."

15 They fell in love and spent the next three weeks together. Before Olga went home, she and Vladimir promised to write and both said, "I will love you forever." They wrote many letters, but each one came 20 back unopened. After a few years, they both married others.

In 1968, Olga came to Canada. In 1985, Vladimir's second marriage was falling apart so he 25 went to Czechoslovakia to look for Olga. Her mother told him that Olga was living in Canada alone! Vladimir decided to immigrate to Canada and to Olga. He waited 30 three years for his papers.

Olga and Vladimir hope to be married by the weekend.

*Instructor's Manual
Original Newspaper Article

DO YOU UNDERSTAND THE STORY?

WHY?

WITH A GROUP

Talk about each question and write a group answer. The answers are not always in the story.*

*1. Why did Olga go home after three weeks in the Soviet Union?

_____

**2. Why did all the letters come back unopened?

_____

*3. Why was Olga living alone in Canada?

_____

*4. Why did Vladimir wait eighteen years before he tried to find Olga?

_____

**5. Why did Vladimir wait three years for his papers?

_____

CLASS DISCUSSION 1

1. What is the best age to get married? Why?
2. How many times do people usually get married in your country?
3. Why do people get divorced?
4. Do many people get divorced in your country?

CLASS DISCUSSION 2

1. Is it easy or difficult to immigrate to Canada?
2. How did you immigrate to Canada?

48

WORDS, WORDS, WORDS!

YOU DON'T NEED A DICTIONARY!

WITH A PARTNER

Often, we can learn the meaning of new words from "clues to meaning" in the sentence or surrounding sentences. Underline the "clues to meaning" for each **new word**.

1. Vladimir worked on a large ship. He was a **sailor**.

2. Vladimir was **tanned** because he was always out in the sun.

3. Vladimir was a very good-looking man. Everyone thought he was very **handsome.**

4. They used their time well. They **spent** every minute together.

5. When you **promise** to do something, you must do it.

6. Their marriage was **falling apart** because they didn't love each other anymore.

7. Olga wasn't living with anyone. She was living **alone**.

8. Olga and Vladimir made the same choice. They **decided** to come and live in Canada.

9. When Olga **immigrated** to Canada, Vladimir had no idea she was leaving Czechoslovakia.

10. **Finally**, after waiting three years, Vladimir received his immigration papers.

WITH A GROUP

Write a definition for each of the new words.

1. sailor: _____

2. tanned: _____

3. handsome: _____

4. spend: _____

5. promise: _____

6. falling apart: _____

7. alone: _____

8. decide: _____

9. immigrate: _____

10. finally: _____

WRITING PRACTICE

CORRECT THE MISTAKES

WITH A PARTNER

Read Vladimir's letter and envelope. Correct all punctuation and capitalization errors.

PUNCTUATION

comma	,
apostrophe	'
period	.
colon	:

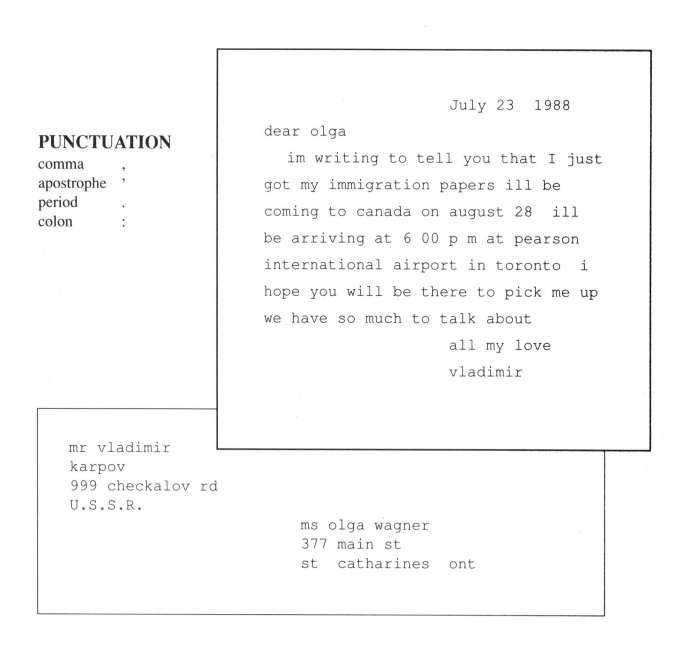

```
                     July 23  1988
dear olga
   im writing to tell you that I just
got my immigration papers ill be
coming to canada on august 28  ill
be arriving at 6 00 p m at pearson
international airport in toronto  i
hope you will be there to pick me up
we have so much to talk about
                     all my love
                     vladimir
```

```
mr vladimir
karpov
999 checkalov rd
U.S.S.R.

              ms olga wagner
              377 main st
              st  catharines  ont
```

WRITING PRACTICE

WRITE A LOVE LETTER

WITH A GROUP

It's August 1, 1988 and you are Olga. Write a letter to Vladimir and address the envelope.

Write your letter and envelope on the blackboard.

YOUR HOMETOWN

WITH A PARTNER

Read about Rosa's hometown, and then write five questions to ask your partner about his/her hometown.

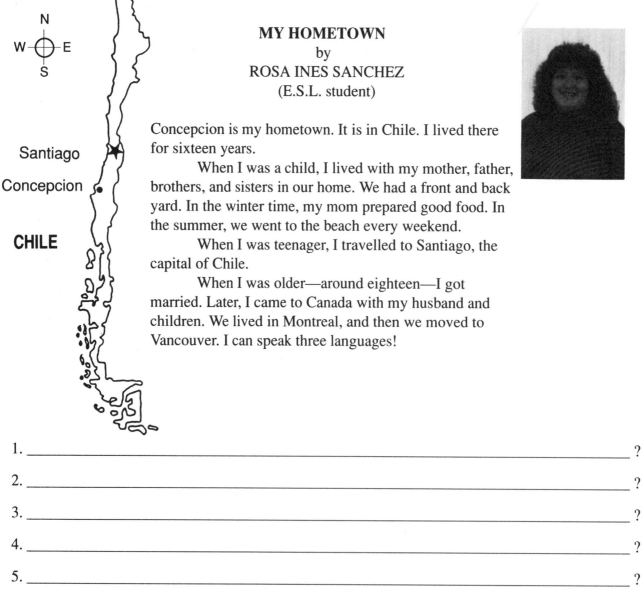

MY HOMETOWN
by
ROSA INES SANCHEZ
(E.S.L. student)

Concepcion is my hometown. It is in Chile. I lived there for sixteen years.

When I was a child, I lived with my mother, father, brothers, and sisters in our home. We had a front and back yard. In the winter time, my mom prepared good food. In the summer, we went to the beach every weekend.

When I was teenager, I travelled to Santiago, the capital of Chile.

When I was older—around eighteen—I got married. Later, I came to Canada with my husband and children. We lived in Montreal, and then we moved to Vancouver. I can speak three languages!

1. _____ ?

2. _____ ?

3. _____ ?

4. _____ ?

5. _____ ?

Show your partner the location of your hometown on the world map.

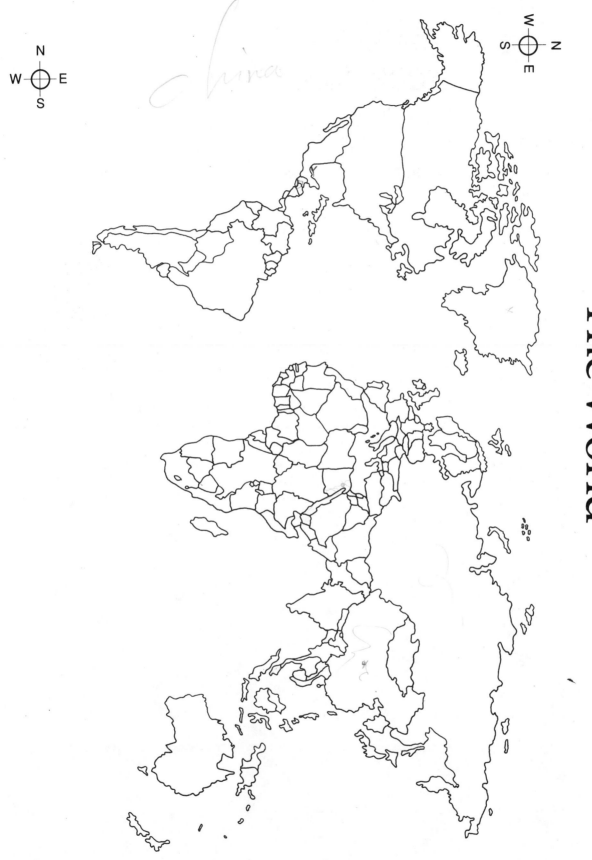

China

The World

CHAPTER 5

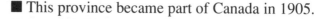

IT HAPPENED IN EDMONTON

FACTS:

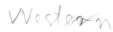

Alberto

★
Edmonton

■ This province became part of Canada in 1905.

■ It is one of the world's greatest oil producers.

■ It is also a leader in grain farming and cattle raising.

■ Summers are warm and sunny. Winters are cold and dry.

■ Edmonton, the capital, has the largest indoor shopping mall in the world.

■ Calgary is the largest city in the province. Edmonton is the second largest.

WITH A GROUP

Find Edmonton on your map of Canada. Answer these questions:

1. Which province is Edmonton in? Write it on the map.

_____

2. Is Edmonton in eastern or western Canada?

_____

3. What do you know about Edmonton?

_____

Western

DESIGN A CLASSIFIED AD

WITH A GROUP

This is a photograph of Noel Desrosier sitting in the back of his truck. Noel is a handyman. He fixes things for other people. He advertises for customers in the newspaper.

Design a newspaper ad for Noel's business.

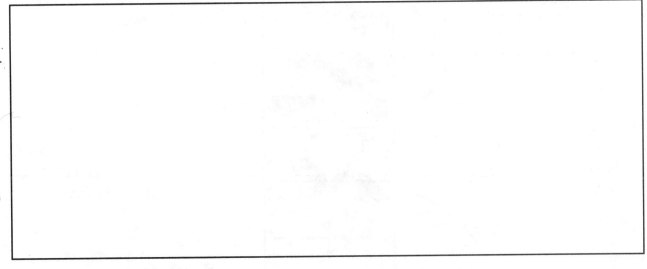

Write your ad on the blackboard.

INTERVIEW: You work for the newspaper

WITH A PARTNER

This is an interview between a newspaper reporter and Noel's best friend. Write the missing words, and then practice the interview. Cover the questions or answers and practice again.

1. What _____ Noel's job?

He _____ a handyman.

2. Where _____ he from?

He _____ from _____ .

3. What _____ he have when he started his business?

He _____ a truck and some tools.

4. What jobs can he _____ ?

He _____ take out garbage and mow lawns.

5. What other jobs _____ he do?

He _____ do plumbing and plastering.

6. What else _____ he do?

He _____ build sundecks and fix electrical wiring.

GETTING READY TO READ

Change roles.

7. What _____ he do when he started his business?

8. What _____ it say?

9. What happened after the ad wo _____ in the paper?

10. What _____ he do then?

11. Who(m) _____ he work for now?

12. How much _____ he charge per visit?

13. Where _____ Noel plan to open companies?

14. What is _____ the name of his company?

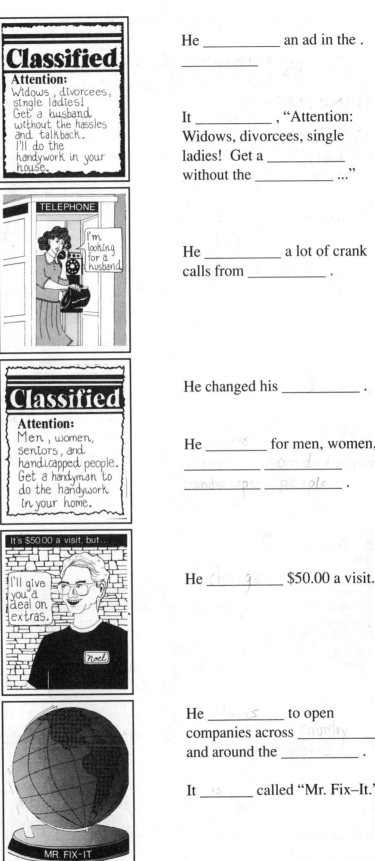

He _____ an ad in the . _____

It _____ , "Attention: Widows, divorcees, single ladies! Get a _____ without the _____ ..."

He _____ a lot of crank calls from _____ .

He changed his _____ .

He _____ for men, women, _____ _____ _____ people .

He changed $50.00 a visit.

He _____ to open companies across country and around the world .

It is _____ called "Mr. Fix–It."

WITH A GROUP Tell the story.

Retell the story with a partner.

What did Noel learn?

June 20

HANDYMAN OR HUSBAND?

1 EDMONTON, ALBERTA — Noel, a handyman from Edmonton, started his "Mr. Fix-It" business with a truck and some tools. He

5 mows lawns and takes out garbage. He also does plumbing and plastering, builds sundecks, and fixes electrical wiring.

2 When he started his business, he

10 wrote a newspaper ad. It read, "Attention: Widows, divorcees, and single ladies! Get a husband without the problems and backtalk. I'll do the handywork in your

15 house," After the ad was in the paper he got a lot of crank calls from women. They thought he wanted to do more than handywork!

3 Now, Noel has a new ad and 20 does household repairs for anyone — men, women, seniors, and handicapped people. He charges a minimum of $50.00 a visit, but if someone doesn't have much 25 money, he gives them a deal on extras.

4 Noel likes his job and wants to open companies in cities across Canada, and possibly, around the 30 world. He would like to become a rich businessman.

*Instructor's Manual
Original Newspaper Article

WHAT'S THE BIG IDEA?

WITH A PARTNER

Choose a title for each paragraph.

Paragraph 1
a) Trucks and Tools
b) Noel's Job X
c) The Garbage Man

Paragraph 2
a) Single Ladies!
b) Noel's Wife
X c) Noel's First Ad

Paragraph 3
X a) Noel's Second Ad
b) Money Talks
c) Household Repairs

Paragraph 4
a) Good Business
b) New Companies
X c) Noel's Future Plans

WHY?

WITH A GROUP

Talk about each question and write a group answer.
The answers are not always in the story.*

**1. Why did Noel start a business?

_____

*2. Why does Noel have a truck?

_____

**3. Why did he write his first ad the way he did?

_____

4. Why did he change his ad?

_____

*5. Why does he give people a deal on extra work?

_____

6. Why does Noel want to open companies in different cities?

_____

WORDS, WORDS, WORDS!

COMPOUND WORDS

Homework is a compound word. It is made from two smaller words: **home** and **work.**

WITH A PARTNER

1. Find eight compound words in the story.
2. Match the words below to make these compounds.
3. Write each compound word in a sentence.

handy	paper	_____
sun	one	_____
any	talk	_____
news	man	*handyman*
handy	deck	_____
some	man	_____
business	work	_____
back	one	_____

1. A _____ fixes things around the house.

2. She wants a husband without the problems and _____ .

3. Noel does _____ for men, women, seniors, and handicapped people.

4. _____ can take out garbage.

5. He put an ad in the _____ .

6. In the summertime, people sit outside on their _____ .

7. Will _____ please fix the kitchen sink!

8. He owns three businesses. He is a _____ .

What other compound words do you know?

_____   _____   _____

_____   _____   _____

READING AND SPEAKING PRACTICE

CLASSIFIED ADS

WITH A PARTNER

1. Read the ads below to find out who these people are talking to. Draw a line from each person to an ad.
2. Practice the conversations.*

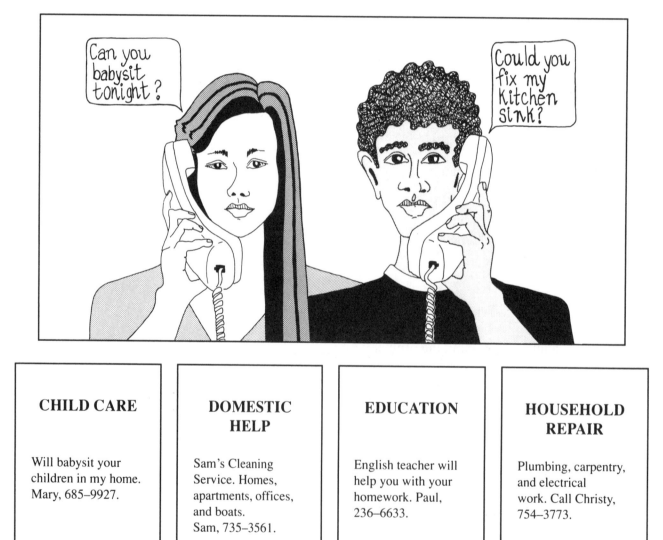

CHILD CARE	DOMESTIC HELP	EDUCATION	HOUSEHOLD REPAIR
Will babysit your children in my home. Mary, 685–9927.	Sam's Cleaning Service. Homes, apartments, offices, and boats. Sam, 735–3561.	English teacher will help you with your homework. Paul, 236–6633.	Plumbing, carpentry, and electrical work. Call Christy, 754–3773.

*Instructor's Manual
Blackboard Dialogue Activity

OPENING YOUR OWN BUSINESS

WITH A GROUP

Think of as many businesses as you can. Think of businesses you would like to open. Write them down. You have five minutes. Use a piece of paper if you need more space.

_____   _____   _____

_____   _____   _____

_____   _____   _____

_____   _____   _____

Share your ideas with the class.

WITH A PARTNER   Interview your partner.

1. What kind of business would you like to open?

   _____

2. What would you call it?

   _____

3. Would you like to have a business partner? Why or why not?

   _____

4. What would you need to start your business?

   _____

5. How many people would you hire?

   _____

6. How much would you pay them?

   _____

7. Where would you open the business?

   _____

8. Where would you advertise?

   _____

EXTRA Write a classified ad for your business on the blackboard.

CHAPTER 6

GETTING READY TO READ

WHAT'S THE STORY?

WITH A GROUP

Look at these newspaper photographs and try to fill in the missing words in the story below. Use your map of Canada to help you.

Sharon Wood, born in Halifax, _____ ^{1} Scotia and raised in Burnaby, British

_____ ^{2} was the first North American _____ ^{3} to climb the 29 028

foot, 8848 _____ ^{4} Mount Everest.

What do you think the rest of the story is about?

IT HAPPENED IN THE ROCKIES

N
W —⊕— E
S

FACTS:

■ The Rocky Mountains run along the border of two western provinces.

■ There are many national parks in this area because it is so beautiful.

■ There are blue–green lakes and snow–capped mountain peaks.

■ The mountains are 2000 to 3900 metres in height.

■ The highest peak is Mount Robson. It is 3954 metres.

WITH A GROUP

Look at your map of Canada and answer these questions.

1. What are the Rockies?

    _____

2. Which provinces are they in? Write the names of these provinces and draw the Rockies on the map above.

    _____

3. How do you think the Rockies got their name?

    _____

4. What do you think Sharon did in the Rockies?

    _____

SHARON WOOD CLIMBS MOUNT EVEREST

WITH THE INSTRUCTOR Answer questions about the pictures and tell the story together.

Retell the story with a partner.

* Instructor's Manual
Simplified Text and Picture Card Masters

Why do you think Sharon climbed Everest?

February 26

LIFE OF A MOUNTAIN CLIMBER

1   GOLDEN, B.C. — Sharon Wood was the youngest of four children. She grew up in B.C. and loved the outdoors. Her father
5   often took her on hikes in the woods. When they came to a hill or a rock, Sharon always climbed it — her father went around!

2   She quit school when she was
10 fifteen, but Mr. Wood wasn't upset. He said "Sharon will find her own way." When she was seventeen, she left home to take a rock-climbing course. Her
15 instructor, Laurie Skreslet, was the first Canadian to climb Mount Everest. Laurie taught her everything he knew about mountain climbing.

When he was finished he said,   20
"She is a better climber than I am."
Sharon said, "Everest is my dream."

In March of 1986, Sharon was   3
in Tibet with a team of twelve   25
Canadians ready to begin their 8848 metre climb. After seven long weeks on the mountain, they only had enough oxygen for two people to go to the top. Sharon   30
Wood and Dwayne Congdon reached the summit on May 20. Sharon was the first Canadian woman to climb Everest. She and Dwayne felt proud as they placed   35
the Canadian flag on top of the world.

*Instructor's Manual
Original Newspaper Article*

DO YOU UNDERSTAND THE STORY?

READING FOR ANSWERS

How fast can you find the answers in the story?

1. How old was Sharon when she quit school?

    _____

2. When did she take her first rock–climbing course?

    _____

3. What year did she climb Everest?

    _____

4. How high is Mount Everest?

    _____

5. How many weeks did it take to climb the mountain?

    _____

6. When did Dwayne and Sharon reach the summit?

    _____

HEADLINES

WITH A GROUP

A headline is a name or title for a newspaper story. Read these headlines and number them starting with the one you think is best.

_____ SEVEN LONG WEEKS   _____ FATHER GOES AROUND

_____ SHARON'S DREAM COMES TRUE   _____ ON TOP OF THE WORLD

_____ SHARON CLIMBS HIGHEST MOUNTAIN   _____ SHARON IS NUMBER ONE

SHARON: CHILD, TEENAGER, AND ADULT

WITH A PARTNER

Which paragraph from the story tells about Sharon as a child?—a teenager?—an adult? Write the number of each paragraph in the spaces below.

CHILD - para. _____	TEENAGER – para. _____	ADULT – para. _____
_____a_____	_____	_____
_____	_____	_____
_____	_____	_____
_____	_____	_____

Read these sentences and write the letters in the spaces above.

a) Sharon played outdoors.

b) Sharon felt proud.

c) She went to Tibet.

d) Sharon was the youngest in her family.

e) She took a rock climbing course.

f) She met Laurie Skreslet.

g) She quit school.

h) She went on hikes with her father.

i) She climbed with Dwayne Congdon.

j) Laurie Skreslet said she was a better climber than he was.

k) She placed the Canadian flag on top of Everest.

l) Sharon lived in B.C.

WORDS, WORDS, WORDS!

YOU DON'T NEED A DICTIONARY!

WITH A PARTNER

Match these words from the story with the underlined words in the sentences below.

a) summit	f) quit
b) upset	g) proud
c) team	h) woods
d) hikes	i) placed
e) instructor	j) outdoors

1. _____ Sharon loved to play <u>outside</u>.

2. _____ Her father liked to go on <u>long walks</u> in the

   _____ <u>forest</u>.

3. _____ When Sharon was fifteen, she <u>stopped going to</u> school.

   _____ but her father wasn't <u>angry</u>.

4. _____ Laurie Skreslet was her <u>teacher</u>.

5. _____ She went to Tibet with a <u>group</u> of Canadian climbers.

6. _____ Dwayne and Sharon felt <u>good about themselves</u>

   _____ when they put the Canadian flag on the <u>top of the</u>

   _____ <u>mountain</u>.

THE CANADIAN FLAG

Canada became a country on July 1, 1867, but Canadians didn't get their own flag until 1965, almost one hundred years later. You may want to know why. The reason is that many Canadians remembered Britain as their homeland and wanted to fly the British flag called the Union Jack.

Union Jack

After the First and Second World Wars, Canadians felt more independent and wanted their own flag. The only problem was that some people wanted a flag with a small Union Jack on it, and others wanted a truly Canadian Flag. The government looked at thousands of different flags and finally decided on the red and white flag we have today. The maple leaf, in the centre, is a symbol of Canada. Canadians think of their country whenever they see it.

Canadian Flag

Where is your homeland? Bring in, or draw a flag of your homeland,
and write a short paragraph about your country.

LANGUAGE PRACTICE

INTERVIEW: You work for the newspaper.

WORK IN GROUPS OF THREE

1. Write questions to ask Sharon. Put the words in order.
2. Practice the interview. One person is a newspaper reporter; one person is Sharon; one person checks the answer key.

1. are – many – there – family – your – children – How – in

_____ ?

2. you – Where – with – did – father – your – go

_____ ?

3. father – climb – hills – and – rocks – Did – to – like – your

_____ ?

4. fifteen – you – when – did – What – do – you – were

_____ ?

5. father – your – Was – angry

_____ ?

6. seventeen – What – you – when – were – you – did – do

_____ ?

Change roles.

7. say – did – about – What – Laurie – your – climbing – Skreslet?

_____?

8. Skreslet – was – Who – Laurie?

_____?

9. was – What – dream – your

_____?

10. did – you – When – to – Mount – begin – climb – Everest

_____?

11. did – Who – climb – you – with

_____?

12. two – go – did – Why – people – only – summit – to – the

_____?

13. on – did – the – you – What – put – summit

_____?

14. was – climb – Why – important – your

_____?

WHAT IS YOUR DREAM?

ON YOUR OWN or WITH A PARTNER

Write your/your partner's answers to these questions and then use the answers to write a paragraph. Then, read the paragraph to a classmate.

1. What is your dream?

   _____

2. Why is this your dream?

   _____

3. How will you accomplish this dream?

   _____

4. Will you be able to accomplish it alone? It not, who will help you?

   _____

5. Do you have other dreams? If so, what are they?

   _____

6. Do you think it's a good idea to dream? Why or why not?

   _____

   _____

   _____

   _____

   _____

   _____

   _____

CHAPTER 7

INUIT VILLAGE : N.W.T.

IT HAPPENED NEAR SPENCE BAY

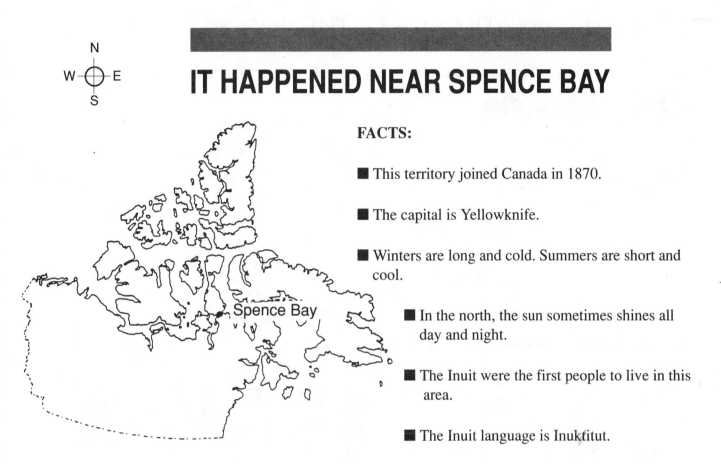

FACTS:

■ This territory joined Canada in 1870.

■ The capital is Yellowknife.

■ Winters are long and cold. Summers are short and cool.

■ In the north, the sun sometimes shines all day and night.

■ The Inuit were the first people to live in this area.

■ The Inuit language is Inuktitut.

WITH A GROUP

Find Spence Bay on your map of Canada. Answer these questions:

1. What part of Canada is Spence Bay in? Write it on the map.

_____

2. What is the weather like in this area?

_____

3. What do you know about the people in this area?

_____

_____

_____

ATIMA GETS THE JOB

WITH THE INSTRUCTOR Answer questions about the pictures and tell the story together.

Retell the story with a partner.

WHAT HAPPENS NEXT?

WITH A PARTNER

Put the sentences in order. Look at the picture story for help. Number one is done for you.

_____ But he stayed in the class and, after a year, he was in Grade 10.

_____ As time went on, he got married and had three children. He needed a better job to support his family.

___1___ Atima grew up in an Inuit village in the Northwest Territories. All of the children went to school by plane.

_____ When he was older, he had problems finding work, and when he did, he could only get low–paying jobs.

_____ He went to the interview and got the job. Today, he translates Inuktitut letters and documents for the government.

_____ On the first day of class, he didn't feel very good. He thought he was too old for school.

_____ One day the plane couldn't land because it was too icy. It never came back and Atima stopped going to school in Grade 3. He never really learned to read or write.

_____ Atima decided to go back to school. He registered in an Adult Upgrading class to study reading, writing, and math.

_____ Atima applied for a job as a translator.

* Instructor's Manual
Simplified Text and Picture Card Masters

What does the headline mean?

March 27

BETTER LATE THAN NEVER

1   SPENCE BAY, N.W.T. — Three years ago, Atima Hadlari had a Grade 3 education. Now, he works as a translator for the
5 Canadian government.

2   The thirty-eight-year-old father of three grew up in an Inuit village near Spence Bay in the Northwest Territories. Every weekday, a
10 plane picked up the children and took them to school. But one day, the plane couldn't land on the ice. It was too dangerous. The plane never returned, and Atima never
15 really learned to read or write. His education ended in Grade 3.

3   When he was a young man, he had trouble finding a good job and never made very much money.
20 After he got married and had children, he decided to do something about this problem. He registered in an Adult Upgrading course to study reading, writing,
25 and math.

4   On the first day of class, Atima didn't feel too good about his decision. He thought he was too old. But he stuck with it, and after a year, he was in Grade 10. He
30 applied for a job as a translator, went to the interview, and got the job!

5   Today, he translates English and Inuktitut letters and documents for
35 the government.

*Instructor's Manual
Original Newspaper Article

WHAT DOES "IT" MEAN?

WITH A PARTNER

Tell what each pronoun refers to.

Paragraph 2
them: _____
it: _____
his: _____

Paragraph 3
this: _____

Paragraph 4
it: _____

WHY?

WITH A GROUP

Talk about each question and write a group answer. The answers are not always in the story.*

**1. Why did the children take a plane to school?

_____

2. Why did Atima's education end in Grade 3?

_____

3. Why did Atima have trouble getting a good job?

_____

4. Why did he register in an Adult Upgrading class?

_____

*5. Why did he stay in school even when he felt old?

_____

*6. Why did he apply for a job as a translator?

_____

WORDS, WORDS, WORDS!

WORD FAMILIES

WITH A PARTNER

Complete the chart with words from the story. Then, fill in the sentences below with the correct form of each word.

	VERB	NOUN
1.	educate	
2.	decide	
3.		registration
4.	translate	
5.		application

1. Atima has a Grade 10 _____ .

   Some people _____ their children at home.

2. Atima _____ to return to school.

   He made a good _____ .

3. Where do I _____ for more English classes?

   It was very busy at _____ yesterday.

4. Atima has a job as a _____ .

   He _____ letters and documents for the government.

5. Can you fill out this job _____ ?

   I want to _____ for a job.

READING AND SPEAKING PRACTICE

THE INUIT

1. Write a word from this story under each picture.
2. Read the information and make up three questions to ask your partner.

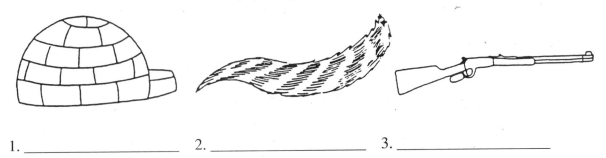

1. _____   2. _____   3. _____

The Inuit are one of Canada's first people. They came here from Siberia and have lived here

for over 4000 years.

In the past, the Inuit lived by hunting, fishing, and food gathering. They travelled around in

groups, looking for food. They made their own clothes and weapons, and slept in igloos or

snowhouses.   5

When they met the white man, life changed little by little. They traded furs for rifles. The

Inuit could kill animals more quickly with their new weapon and soon, there were no more to

kill. They had no way to make a living.

Now, most Inuit live in villages paid for by the government. Some get jobs in construction,

transportation, education, or crafts, but many live on income assistance. The government is   10

trying to help these people find new ways to live.

_____?

_____?

_____?

FILLING OUT AN APPLICATION

WITH A PARTNER

Ask your partner questions and fill in his/her application form. Check the answer key if you don't know how to ask any of the questions.

JOB APPLICATION		
1. Family Name	2. Given Name	3. Middle Name
4. Address		
5. City	6. Province	
7. Country	8. Postal Code	
9. Residence Phone	10. Business Phone	
11. Social Insurance Number	12. Date of Birth	
13. Education — Last Grade Completed 1 2 3 4 5 6 7 8 9 10 11 12		
14. Other Training		
15. Languages Spoken	16. Languages Written	
17. Previous Employment — Position — Name of Company		
18. Address		
19. References — Name	Address	
1.		
2.		
20. Date	21. Signature	

t questions are illegal on job application forms?

YOUR JOBS: PAST AND FUTURE

WITH A PARTNER

Ask your partner about a job she/he had.

1. What kind of job did you have?

   _____

2. What did you do? (What were your duties?)

   _____

3. Where did you work?

   _____

4. What were your hours?

   _____

5. What kind of boss did you have?

   _____

6. Who(m) did you work with? Were they friendly?

   _____

7. Did you get a vacation? How long was it? Where did you go?

   _____

8. Did you get any benefits? If yes, what kind?

   _____

9. How long did you work there?

   _____

10. Why did you leave?

    _____

11. What kind of job would you like to have in the future?

    _____

12. Do you want to go back to school for any retraining?

    _____

LISTENING AND SPEAKING PRACTICE

PREPARING FOR AN INTERVIEW

WITH A PARTNER

1. Decide on a job you would like to apply for.
2. Make up questions you think the boss might ask.
3. Write questions you would like to ask.
4. Practice the interview.

JOB: _____

BOSS: Good morning. I was just reading your application. Please sit down.

YOU: Thank you

Boss's Questions

1. _____?
2. _____?
3. _____?
4. _____?
5. _____?

Your Questions

1. _____?
2. _____?
3. _____?
4. _____?
5. _____?

*Instructor's Manual
Blackboard Dialogue Activity

WHAT ABOUT YOU?

AT THE INTERVIEW

WITH A GROUP

How should you act during an interview? Check an answer and write the reason why.

SHOULD YOU ...

		Yes	No	It Depends	
1.	arrive early?	❏	❏	❏	_____
2.	shake hands?	❏	❏	❏	_____
3.	call the interviewer by his/her first name?	❏	❏	❏	_____
4.	not answer a question?	❏	❏	❏	_____
5.	speak your language?	❏	❏	❏	_____
6.	bring a resume?	❏	❏	❏	_____
7.	bring a friend?	❏	❏	❏	_____
8.	chew gum?	❏	❏	❏	_____
9.	smile a lot?	❏	❏	❏	_____
10.	look the interviewer in the eyes?	❏	❏	❏	_____
11.	say you really need the job?	❏	❏	❏	_____
12.	ask a lot of questions?	❏	❏	❏	_____
13.	say, "My English is bad."?	❏	❏	❏	_____
14.	say you don't understand?	❏	❏	❏	_____
15.	say you don't know?	❏	❏	❏	_____

CHAPTER 8

WHAT DO YOU LIKE DOING IN YOUR FREE TIME?

WITH A PARTNER

Complete the words which describe free–time activities. Then talk about what you like and don't like doing in your free time. Ask other questions to find out more information. For example, "Why," "Where," "How often," etc.

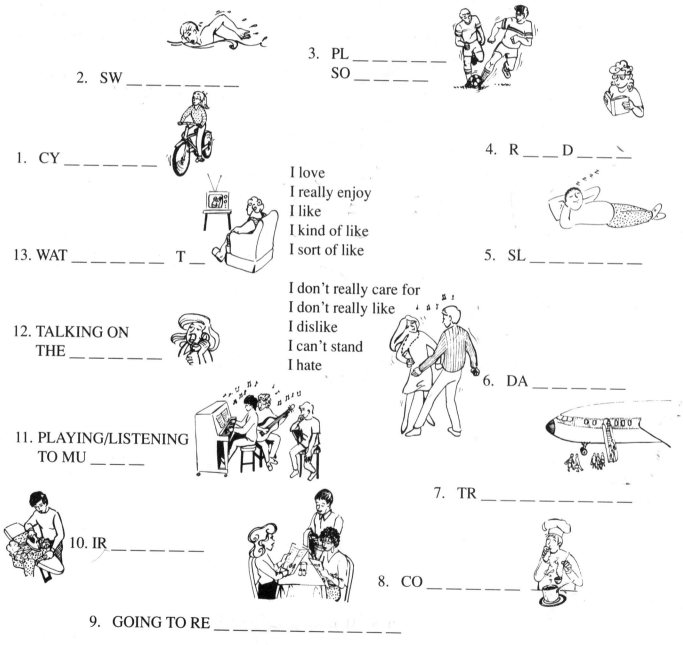

2. SW _ _ _ _ _ _ _ _

3. PL _ _ _ _ _ _ _
   SO _ _ _ _ _

1. CY _ _ _ _ _ _ _

4. R _ _ D _ _ _ _

13. WAT _ _ _ _ _ _ T _

I love
I really enjoy
I like
I kind of like
I sort of like

5. SL _ _ _ _ _ _ _ _

12. TALKING ON
    THE _ _ _ _ _ _

I don't really care for
I don't really like
I dislike
I can't stand
I hate

6. DA _ _ _ _ _ _ _

11. PLAYING/LISTENING
    TO MU _ _ _

7. TR _ _ _ _ _ _ _ _ _ _

10. IR _ _ _ _ _ _ _

8. CO _ _ _ _ _ _ _

9. GOING TO RE _ _ _ _ _ _ _ _ _ _ _ _

IT HAPPENED IN OTTAWA

Ottawa

FACTS:

■ This was one of Canada's first four provinces.

■ One third of Canada's people live in this province.

■ Ottawa lies on the Ottawa River in the southeastern part of this province.

■ Ottawa is the capital of Canada.

■ Most people in Ottawa work for the federal government.

■ In the winter, Ottawans can skate outdoors on the Rideau Canal.

WITH A GROUP

Find Ottawa on your map of Canada. Answer these questions:

1. Which province is Ottawa in? Write it on the map.

_____

2. What is important about this city?

_____

3. What languages do people in Ottawa speak?

_____

4. What do you think people from Ottawa do in their free time?

_____

WHAT'S THE STORY?

WITH A GROUP

Look at this newspaper photograph and read the caption.
Answer the questions.

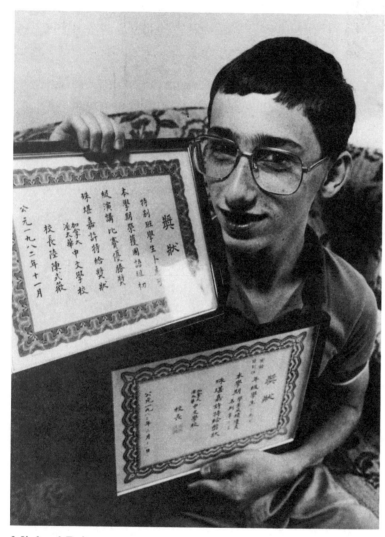

Michael Britton
A taste for different things.

1. What is Michael holding?

   _____

2. What language do you see?

   _____

3. What do you think Michael learned
   to do in his free time?

   _____

   _____

4. Do you think he has any other
   hobbies? If so, what?

   _____

   _____

   _____

CANADIAN LEARNS CHINESE

WITH THE INSTRUCTOR Answer questions about the pictures and tell the story together.

Retell the story with a partner..

* Instructor's Manual
Simplified Text and Picture Card Masters

How did Michael learn Chinese?

June 3

CANADIAN GRADUATES FROM CHINESE SCHOOL

1 OTTAWA, ONTARIO — Six years ago, Michael Britton, a high school student from Ottawa, told his parents he

2 10 wanted to learn Chinese in his free time. They were surprised and said, "It will be difficult for you because all the other students will have one or two Chinese parents."

15 Michael wasn't worried. He liked a challenge and spent the next six years learning Mandarin, the official language of China. He went

3 to language class every Saturday

20 morning. In the afternoon, he learned about Chinese culture by making crafts, playing ping-pong, and practicing kung-fu.

Michael said the most difficult part was learning to write the 25 language. Each word has its own symbol and you have to remember every one. He knows 2000 Chinese 4 characters and can write 1000.

Michael graduated with a 75% 30 average. He wanted a higher mark but all the other students had Chinese parents to practice with. Michael's teachers made him tapes and he used his English-Chinese 35 dictionary to learn new words. He was the first non-Chinese student to graduate from the school.

Chinese is not Michael's only 5 hobby. He also studies French, 40 speaks a little German, plays the recorder, collects stamps and coins, and is interested in science.

*Instructor's Manual
Original Newspaper Article*

98

DO YOU UNDERSTAND THE STORY?

READING FOR ANSWERS

How fast can you find the answers in the story? Circle the correct answers.

1. How many years did Michael study Chinese?

   a) ten years   b) two years   c) six years ✓

2. Which day of the week did he study?

   a) Friday   b) Saturday ✓   c) Sunday

3. How many symbols does he know?

   a) 1000   b) 2000 ✓   c) 3000

4. What was his final mark?

   a) 65   b) 70   c) 75 ´

5. How many languages does Michael know?

   a) 4   b) 3   c) 2

WHY?

WITH A GROUP

Talk about each question and write a group answer. The answers are not always in the story.*

*1. Why did Michael want to learn Chinese?

_____

2. Why did his parents say, "It will be difficult."?

_____

3. Why did Michael find the language difficult?

_____

4. Why did Michael make crafts, play ping–pong and practice kung–fu?

_____

**5. Why did he want a higher mark?

_____

*6. Why is Michael interesting?

_____

DO YOU UNDERSTAND THE STORY?

ON SATURDAY

WITH A PARTNER

Reread the story and fill in the chart with activities Michael does on Saturday morning, afternoon and evening. Then, ask your partner what she/he usually does on Saturday.

	Michael	Your Partner
M O R N I N G	1. 2. 3. 4.	1. 2. 3. 4.
A F T E R N O O N	1. 2. 3. 4.	1. 2. 3. 4.
E V E N I N G	1. 2. 3. 4.	1. 2. 3. 4.

WORDS, WORDS, WORDS!

CROSSWORD PUZZLE

WITH A GROUP

Read the clues and write words from the story in the puzzle.

ACROSS

1. When a mother can't find her child, she gets
   _____ .

4. A ___hobby___ is something you do
   you your free time.

7. People with many different
   _____ live in Canada.

9. Every word in Chinese has a different
   _____ .

10. Learning Chinese was _____
    for Michael.

DOWN

2. Canada has two ___official___
   languages.

3. If you like to do something difficult, then
   you like a _____ .

5. Michael _____ with a 75%
   average.

6. _____ is the official language
   of China.

7. Making things with your hands is called
   making _____ .

8. Every word in Chinese has a different
   character or _____ .

101

CANADA HAS TWO OFFICIAL LANGUAGES

Read the information below to answer the following questions:

1. What are Canada's two official languages?

   _____

2. How many Canadians speak English as their first language?

   _____

3. How many Canadians speak French as their first language?

   _____

4. Where do most French Canadians live?

   _____

5. Where can Canadians speak either official language?

   _____

6. Why do many Canadians learn to speak both French and English?

   _____

Canada has two official languages: English and French. Over fifteen million people speak English as their first language and more than six million people speak French. Of these French–speaking Canadians, approximately five million live in Quebec.

Because French and English are the official languages, all federal laws are written in both languages. Canadians can use either language in federal courts of law and have the right to be served in French or English when using a federal government service such as the Post Office, the Immigration Office, the Unemployment Insurance Commission Office, or the Motor Vehicle Department.

Many Canadians learn to speak both official languages. They want to be bilingual so they can communicate with other Canadians and learn about their culture.

LEARNING A LANGUAGE

INTERVIEW YOUR PARTNER

1. Where do you study English?

    _____

2. How many hours a week do you study?

    _____

3. How do you learn the language?

    _____

4. What do you do to learn outside of class?

    _____

5. What is the easiest part of learning the language?

    _____

6. What is difficult about learning English?

    _____

7. What other language(s) do you speak?

    _____

INTERVIEW A CANADIAN

1. Where were you born?

    _____

2. How many languages do you speak?

    _____

3. Do you want to learn another language? If so, which one?

    _____

4. Would you like to learn French? Why or why not?

    _____

5. What is the difference between the French and English Canadian culture?

    _____

CHAPTER 9

LOBSTER TRAPPING: N.S.

30 Lobsters
To: Vancouver

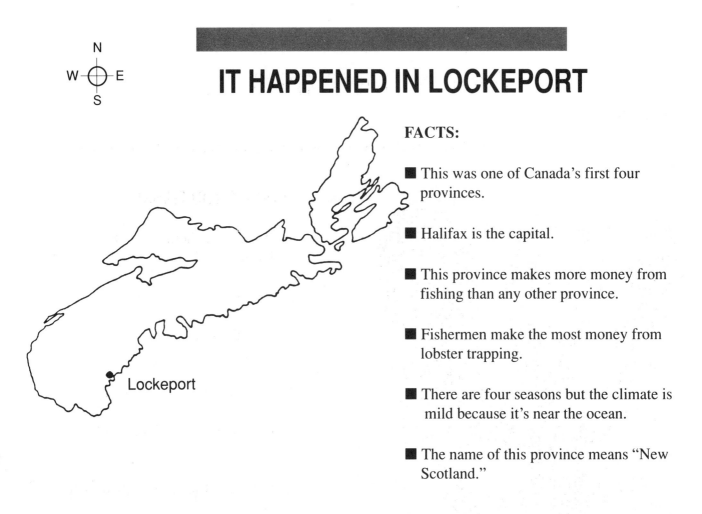

IT HAPPENED IN LOCKEPORT

Lockeport

FACTS:

■ This was one of Canada's first four provinces.

■ Halifax is the capital.

■ This province makes more money from fishing than any other province.

■ Fishermen make the most money from lobster trapping.

■ There are four seasons but the climate is mild because it's near the ocean.

■ The name of this province means "New Scotland."

WITH A GROUP

Find Lockeport on your map of Canada. Answer these questions:

1. Which province is Lockeport in? Write it on the map.

    _____

2. Which ocean surrounds this province?

    _____

3. What is the name for the group of four small provinces in this area?

    _____

4. What kind of work do people do in this area?

    _____

WHAT'S THE STORY?

WITH A GROUP

This is a newspaper photograph of Wylie, a B.C. lobster wholesaler and Loretta, the lobster. Look at the picture and discuss the questions.

WHAT DO YOU THINK?

1. Where do fishermen catch lobsters?

2. Where does Wylie work?

3. Why does the lobster have a name?

4. Is Wylie going to sell Loretta?

5. Can lobsters live in the Pacific Ocean?

6. How does Canadian Airlines help Wylie?

Tell the story.

_____

_____

_____

_____

_____

UNDERSTANDING THE STORY

LORETTA LOBSTER FLIES HOME

WITH THE INSTRUCTOR Answer questions about the pictures and tell the story together.

Retell the story with a partner.

Why did Wylie set Loretta free?

July 1

FREE AT LAST

1   LOCKEPORT, N.S. — Wylie Costain, a B.C. lobster wholesaler, brought a giant lobster back to Nova Scotia today and set her free in the Atlantic Ocean.

2   Thousands of lobsters live in the cold Atlantic waters off the coast of this province and lobster trapping is a big industry. Fishermen catch the lobsters using special wooden traps, pack about thirty to a crate, and then send them to cities around the world.

3   Last week in British Columbia, Wylie was opening one of these crates. He was very surprised when he found one huge lobster packed into a single crate. It weighed nine and a half kilograms or twenty-one pounds.

4   Wylie kept the lobster and showed it to his friend. This man was a lobster expert; he knew everything about lobsters. He said the lobster was 147 years old, a female and in perfect condition. They called the lobster Loretta.

5   Wylie didn't want anyone to eat Loretta for dinner. She was a special lobster because she was so old. Wylie wanted to set her free. His friend said, "Loretta won't be happy here in the Pacific Ocean. She has to go back to her home in the Atlantic."

6   Wylie called Canadian Airlines and they offered to fly both him and Loretta to Nova Scotia free of charge. Wylie packed Loretta in a special crate and they flew over 4000 kilometres to Nova Scotia.

7   Before he let her swim away, Wylie said, "Good-bye Loretta," and gave her a big hug. Then he put her in the water, and she swam happily into the sea.

What is special about the date of this newspaper story?

*Instructor's Manual
Original Newspaper Article

WHAT'S THE BIG IDEA?

WITH A PARTNER

Reread the story to find the main idea (most important idea) in each of the following paragraphs. Circle the correct answer.

Paragraph 2
a) Lobster trapping is a big industry in Nova Scotia.
b) Fishermen catch lobsters in wooden traps.
c) Fishermen send lobsters to different cities around the world.

Paragraph 3
a) Wylie was opening a crate.
b) He was surprised to find a huge lobster.
c) The lobster weighed 9.5 kilograms.

Paragraph 4
a) Wylie's friend is a lobster expert.
b) The lobster expert examined (looked at) the lobster.
c) They called the lobster Loretta.

Paragraph 5
a) Wylie didn't want anyone to eat Loretta for dinner.
b) Wylie wanted to set Loretta free.
c) The expert said, "She has to go back to the Atlantic."

Paragraph 6
a) Wylie called Canadian Airlines.
b) Canadian Airlines offered to fly Wylie and Loretta to Nova Scotia free of charge.
c) They flew to Nova Scotia.

Paragraph 7
a) Wylie said, "Good–bye Loretta."
b) Wylie hugged Loretta.
c) Loretta was happy to be home.

WHAT'S THE BIG IDEA?

WITH A PARTNER

Reread the story to find the main idea (most important idea) in each of the following paragraphs. Circle the correct answer.

Paragraph 2
a) Lobster trapping is a big industry in Nova Scotia.
b) Fishermen catch lobsters in wooden traps.
c) Fishermen send lobsters to different cities around the world.

Paragraph 3
a) Wylie was opening a crate.
b) He was surprised to find a huge lobster.
c) The lobster weighed 9.5 kilograms.

Paragraph 4
a) Wylie's friend is a lobster expert.
b) The lobster expert examined (looked at) the lobster.
c) They called the lobster Loretta.

Paragraph 5
a) Wylie didn't want anyone to eat Loretta for dinner.
b) Wylie wanted to set Loretta free.
c) The expert said, "She has to go back to the Atlantic."

Paragraph 6
a) Wylie called Canadian Airlines.
b) Canadian Airlines offered to fly Wylie and Loretta to Nova Scotia free of charge.
c) They flew to Nova Scotia.

Paragraph 7
a) Wylie said, "Good–bye Loretta."
b) Wylie hugged Loretta.
c) Loretta was happy to be home.

WHAT'S THE STORY?

WITH A GROUP

This is a newspaper photograph of Wylie, a B.C. lobster wholesaler and Loretta, the lobster. Look at the picture and discuss the questions.

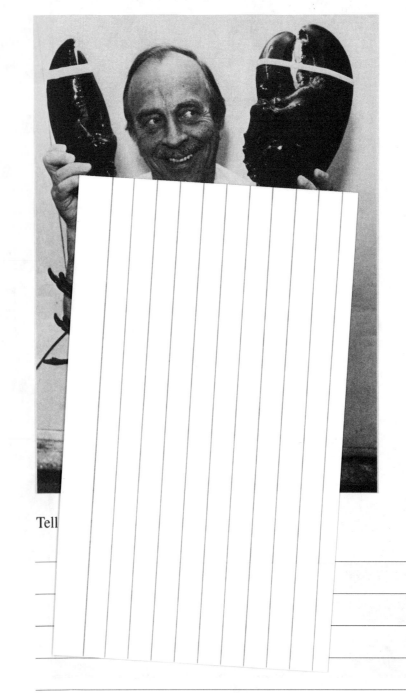

WHAT DO YOU THINK?

1. Where do fishermen catch lobsters?

2. Where does Wylie work?

3. Why does the lobster have a name?

4. Is Wylie going to sell Loretta?

5. Can lobsters live in the Pacific Ocean?

6. How does Canadian Airlines help Wylie?

Tell

▇ LORETTA LOBSTER FLIES HOME ▇

WITH THE INSTRUCTOR Answer questions about the pictures and tell the story together.

Retell the story with a partner.

* Instructor's Manual
Simplified Text and Picture Card Masters

Why did Wylie set Loretta free?

July 1

FREE AT LAST

1   LOCKEPORT, N.S. — Wylie Costain, a B.C. lobster wholesaler, brought a giant lobster back to Nova Scotia today and set her free

5   in the Atlantic Ocean.

2   Thousands of lobsters live in the cold Atlantic waters off the coast of this province and lobster trapping is a big industry.

10   Fishermen catch the lobsters using special wooden traps, pack about thirty to a crate, and then send them to cities around the world.

Last week in British Columbia,

3 15 Wylie was opening one of these crates. He was very surprised when he found one huge lobster packed into a single crate. It weighed nine and a half kilograms or twenty-one

20   pounds.

Wylie kept the lobster and showed it to his friend. This man was a lobster expert; he knew

4

everything about lobsters. He said the lobster was 147 years old, a female and in perfect condition. They called the lobster Loretta.

Wylie didn't want anyone to eat Loretta for dinner. She was a special lobster because she was so old. Wylie wanted to set her free. His friend said, "Loretta won't be happy here in the Pacific Ocean. She has to go back to her home in the Atlantic."

Wylie called Canadian Airlines and they offered to fly both him and Loretta to Nova Scotia free of charge. Wylie packed Loretta in a special crate and they flew over 4000 kilometres to Nova Scotia.

Before he let her swim away, Wylie said, "Good-bye Loretta," and gave her a big hug. Then he put her in the water, and she swam happily into the sea.

What is special about the date of this newspaper story?

*Instructor's Manual
Original Newspaper Art

WORDS THAT GO TOGETHER

WITH A PARTNER

Which words go together? Write the words, and then put them in the sentences below.

wooden	trapping	_____
lobster	waters	_____
huge	expert	_____
perfect	free	_____
set (her)	traps	*wooden traps*
free	lobster	_____
lobster	condition	_____
swim	wholesaler	_____
Atlantic	of charge	_____
lobster	away	_____

1. Loretta was a big lobster; in fact, she was a _____ _____ .

2. Wylie's friend knew everything about lobsters. He was a _____ _____ .

3. Wylie put Loretta into the water and let her _____ _____ .

4. Loretta was in good health. She was in _____ _____ .

5. Wylie sells lobsters to stores and restaurants. He is a _____ _____ .

6. _____ _____ is a Canadian industry.

7. Lobsters like the cold _____ _____ .

8. Fishermen catch lobsters with _____ _____ .

9. Wylie did not pay for his airline ticket. He flew _____ _____ _____ .

10. Wylie did not want to sell Loretta. He wanted to _____ _____ _____

READING AND SPEAKING PRACTICE

THE YELLOW PAGES

WITH A PARTNER

Find the number each of these people should call. Then, practice the conversations.

1. Wylie has a problem.

   Number: _____641-2111_____

2. When Betty arrived home from her holiday, her suitcase didn't. It was missing.

   Number: _____

3. Jack wants to send a bicycle to his brother in Poland.

   Number: _____

4. Leslie is planning a trip to Seoul, Korea. She wants some information.

   Number: _____

5. Gerry wants to know what time his father's plane from Edmonton is arriving.

   Number: _____

6. Linda wants to make reservations for five people to fly from Ottawa to Regina next Saturday. Three small children and two adults will be flying.

   Number: _____

Canadi>n

Bringing more Canadians
to more places
in Canada
and the world
than any other airline

PASSENGER SERVICES
Canadian Airlines International
  Reservations ----------------- 682-1411

ARRIVAL & DEPARTURE INFORMATION
CANADIAN AIRLINES INTERNATIONAL
  Flight Arrival & Departure Information
  (24 Hour Service) ------------- 689-9166

BAGGAGE SERVICES
CANADIAN AIRLINES INTERNATIONAL
  ------------------------- 276-7310

TICKET OFFICES
CANADIAN AIRLINES INTERNATIONAL
  1004 W Georgia -------------- 682-1411
  200-601 W Cordova ---------- 682-1411
  300-999 Canada Place -------- 682-1411
  10251 St Edwards Rmd -------- 682-1411

DISTRICT SALES OFFICE
CANADIAN AIRLINES INTERNATIONAL
  205-601 W Cordova ----------- 641-2700

CHARTER SALES OFFICE
CANADIAN AIRLINES INTERNATIONAL
  Passenger Sales
  1 Grant Mcconachie Way Rmd -- 270-5211

AIR CARGO SERVICES
CANADIAN AIRLINES INTERNATIONAL
  Cargo Information & Rates ------- 278-2131
  Pickup & Delivery Mon to Fri 8:00 am
  to 5:00 pm ---------------- 278-2131
  Cargo Sales
  4840 Miller Rd Rmd --------- 270-5130

ADMINISTRATIVE OFFICES
CANADIAN AIRLINES INTERNATIONAL
  1 Grant Mcconachie Way Rmd ---- 270-5521
  Canadian Plus ---------------- 266-1717
  Luggage Centre
  7771 Alderbridge Way--------- 270-5775

EXECUTIVE OFFICES
CANADIAN AIRLINES INTERNATIONAL
  1055 Dunsmuir --------------- 641-2000
  Public Relations -------------- 641-2111

CANADIAN INDUSTRY

Read the information below to answer the following questions:

1. What are two of Canada's oldest industries?

   _____

2. Where do most Canadians work today?

   _____

3. Which industry employs seventy percent of Canadian workers?

   _____

4. What is the second biggest industry in Canada?

   _____

5. What are the other important industries?

   _____

When we think of Canadian industry, we think of fishing and farming. It is true that these are Canada's oldest industries, but today they only employ about 5% of the total population. Today, the majority of Canadians work in big cities like Toronto, Montreal, or Edmonton. They work in restaurants, hospitals, offices, stores, schools, and banks. These people are part of the large service industry which employs seventy percent of all workers.

The second largest industry is manufacturing. Approximately eighteen percent of the population work in factories and make things. Some make automobiles for trade to the U.S. and others process foods: they pack meats or can fruits and vegetables.

Other important industries include mining, construction, farming, forestry, and fishing. They employ twelve percent of Canadian workers.

Tell about the important industries in your country.

FISHING AND COOKING

WITH A GROUP

Interview a student who has gone fishing. Ask these and any other questions you can think of. Use the answers to write a "group story" about the fishing trip.

1. Do you like fishing? Why or why not?
2. When did you last go fishing?
3. Where did you go fishing?
4. Who did you go with?
5. How long did you stay?
6. How many fish did you catch?
7. What kind of fish did you catch?
8. How big was the biggest fish you ever caught?
9. How did you cook it?
10. How did it taste?

WITH A PARTNER

Ask your partner to tell you a good recipe for fish.

Name of recipe: _____

Ingredients

_____   _____   _____

_____   _____   _____

_____   _____   _____

Method

_____

_____

_____

_____

CHAPTER 10

WHAT'S THE QUESTION?

Skim the answers to find out what question these students are answering.

Joszef Kovacs
Hungary
I would buy a beautiful house for my mother, and then buy a new sports car.

Annie Tang
China
I would give all the money to disabled people.

Shughi Gerami
Iran
I would buy two restaurants, get married, visit my country, and buy a new car.

Thi Mai Dang Huynh
Vietnam
I would give some money to charity, bring my family to Canada, and then I would go to a beauty shop!

Aziz Azmand
Iran
I would give half to hungry people, and build a school for the poor with the other half.

Julia Rivero
Nicaragua
I would pay my debts and be thankful to God for the rest of my life.

Write the question _____?

WHAT WOULD YOU DO IF...?

WITH THE CLASS

Ask the same question to five people in your class. Write their answers.

1. Name: _____

   Answer: _____

   _____

3. Name: _____

   Answer: _____

   _____

4. Name: _____

   Answer: _____

   _____

5. Name: _____

   Answer: _____

   _____

Share your answers with a partner and then discuss these question with the class.

CLASS DISCUSSION

1. Do you buy lottery tickets?
2. What kind do you buy?
3. How much do the tickets cost?
4. Did you ever win any money?
5. What numbers are lucky for you? Why?
6. Do you think lotteries are good or bad for people? Why?
7. Can you buy lottery tickets in your country?

WHAT'S THE STORY?

WITH A GROUP

This newspaper photograph shows Jean–Guy Lavigueur kissing William Murphy. Discuss these questions.

1. Why is Jean–Guy kissing William?
2. Why is William smiling?

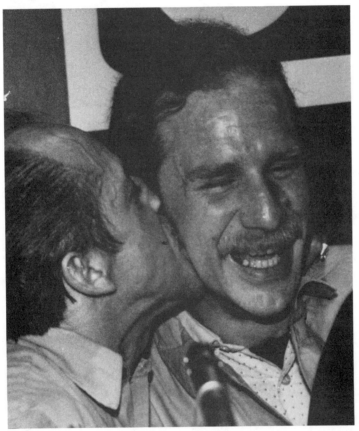

Twenty Questions

Ask your instructor twenty "Yes/No" questions to find out more about this interesting newspaper story.
What do you think the story is about?

_____

_____

_____

_____

IT HAPPENED IN MONTREAL

FACTS:

■ This was one of Canada's first four provinces.

■ Quebec City is the capital.

■ It's Canada's largest province.

■ Most people speak French as their first language.

■ Summers are hot and humid. Winters are long and cold.

■ The name of the province comes from the Algonquian Indian name "Kebec" meaning "place where the river narrows."

WITH A GROUP

Find Montreal on your map of Canada. Answer these questions.

1. Which province is Montreal in?

_____

2. How far is Montreal from where you live?

_____

3. What do you know about Montreal?

_____

4. What languages do Montrealers speak?

_____

HONEST TICKET–FINDER GETS $1.2 MILLION

WITH THE INSTRUCTOR Answer questions about the pictures and tell the story together.

Retell the story with a partner.

* Instructor's Manual
Simplified Text and Picture Card Masters

Do you think William's life will improve?

April 2

HONESTY PAYS

MONTREAL, QUEBEC — William Murphy had fifty-six cents in the bank, lived in a small room, and was unemployed. But, he had
5   one thing going for him. He was honest. And that honesty paid off for him yesterday. He received a 1.2-million cheque for returning a lost lottery ticket to the owner.

10   Last Sunday morning, Murphy found a wallet while he was walking down the street. He picked it up and looked inside. He found I.D. cards, $18.00, and six lottery tickets. He
15   checked the identification and saw that the wallet belonged to Mr. Jean-Guy Lavigueur.

He put the wallet in the mailbox but he kept the lottery tickets. He
20   thought, "Maybe, I'll win $10.00 or something."

Later that evening, he checked the newspaper. He had the winning lottery ticket and it was worth $7
25   650 267.00. He was so surprised he almost had a heart attack!

For a minute, he thought about keeping the ticket but then decided to return it to Mr. Lavigueur. He remembered the address from the I.D. cards so he went to the house   30
and knocked on the door.

Yves, Jean-Guy's French-speaking son answered the door. William tried to tell him about the lottery ticket but Yves didn't   35
understand a word of English. Yves told him to go away in French. Then, he closed the door in William's face!

The next night, William returned with a bilingual friend. This time,   40
Jean-Guy opened the door. William gave him the ticket and said, "You are a millionaire! This is your ticket and it's worth over $7 million."

Jean-Guy said, "You are an honest   45
man. I'm giving you a $1.2-million reward."

Both men are very happy. Jean-Guy is going to share the money with his family. They are going to buy a   50
new house. William Murphy plans to go skiing in Vancouver.

---

*Instructor's Manual
Original Newspaper Article

WHAT DOES "IT" MEAN?

WITH A PARTNER

Read these paragraphs from the story. All of the pronouns are circled. Draw a line from each pronoun to the name of the person or thing it means.

The next night, William returned with a bilingual friend. This time, Jean–Guy opened the door. William gave (him) the ticket and said, ("You) are a millionaire! This is (your) ticket and (it)'s worth over $7 million."

Jean–Guy said, ("You) are an honest man. (I)'m giving you a $1.2 million dollar reward."

Both men were very happy. Jean-Guy is going to share the money with (his) family. (They) are going to buy a new house. William plans to go skiing in Vancouver.

READING FOR ANSWERS

WITH A PARTNER

How fast can you find the answers in the story?

1. What did William receive for his honesty?

   _____ _____ - _____ _____

2. What are the full names of the three people in the story?

   a) _____ b) _____ c) _____

3. When did William find the wallet?

   _____ _____ _____

4. What was inside the wallet?

   _____ , _____ _____ and _____ _____ _____

5. How much was the winning ticket worth?

   _____

DO YOU UNDERSTAND THE STORY?

MIXED FEELINGS

WITH A GROUP

Talk about how William felt in the following situations.
Give a reason for your answer(s).

1. William was unemployed, lived in a small room and had fifty-six cents in the bank.
   a) content   b) depressed   c) hopeful

2. He found a wallet on the street.
   a) surprised   b) curious   c) lucky

3. He put the wallet in the mailbox but he kept the tickets.
   a) helpful   b) honest   c) dishonest

4. He had the winning lottery ticket.
   a) happy   b) worried   c) indecisive

5. He decided to return the ticket.
   a) calm   b) poor   c) decisive

6. Yves closed the door in his face.
   a) angry   b) happy   c) frustrated

7. William returns to the Lavigueur home with a bilingual friend.
   a) persistent   b) intelligent   c) generous

8. William gives Jean-Guy the winning ticket.
   a) stupid   b) honest   c) dishonest

9. Jean-Guy gives William a reward.
   a) angry   b) thrilled   c) rich

10. William plans to go skiing in Vancouver.
    a) carefree   b) energetic   c) lazy

Talk about other adjectives to describe people. Which adjectives describe you?

WORD FAMILIES

WITH A PARTNER

Complete the chart with words from the story. Then fill in the sentences with the correct form of each word.

	VERB	NOUN	ADJECTIVE
1.		winner	
2.	—		million
3.	rewarded		rewarding
4.	—		honest
5.		memory	memorable
6.		belongings	—
7.		decision	decisive

1. Jean–Guy was a lottery _____ .

   William found the _____ ticket.

2. The ticket was worth over $7 _____ .

   Jean–Guy is a multi– _____ .

3. William got a large _____ .

   Jean–Guy _____ him for his honesty.

4. Jean–Guy feels that _____ is important.

   William is an _____ man.

5. William _____ the address.

   He has a good _____ .

6. Jean–Guy lost one of his important _____ .

   The lottery tickets _____ to Jean–Guy.

INTERVIEW: You work for the newspaper.

WORK IN GROUPS OF THREE

One person is the newspaper reporter and makes questions to ask William Murphy. One person is William Murphy and answers the questions. The third person checks the answer key.

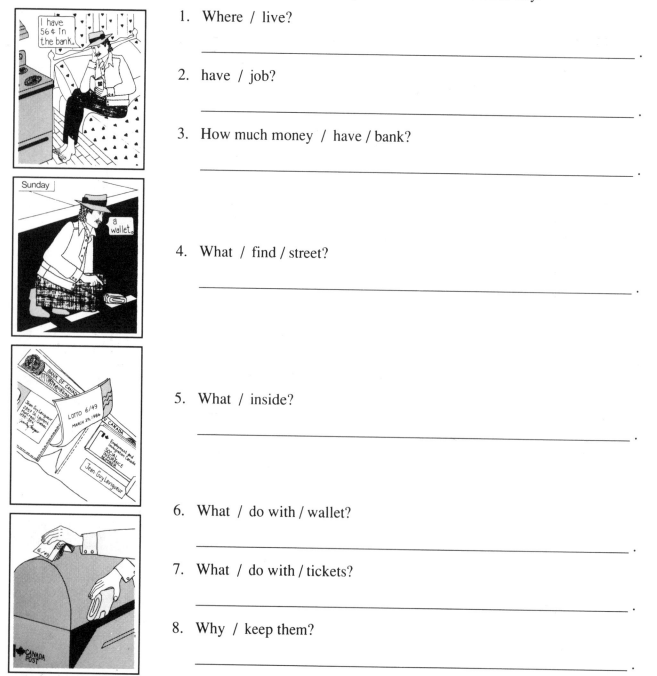

1. Where / live?

   _____.

2. have / job?

   _____.

3. How much money / have / bank?

   _____.

4. What / find / street?

   _____.

5. What / inside?

   _____.

6. What / do with / wallet?

   _____.

7. What / do with / tickets?

   _____.

8. Why / keep them?

   _____.

Change roles.

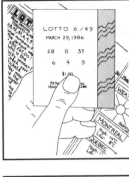

9. Where / check / lottery numbers?

_____ .

10. How / feel?

_____ .

11. What / decide / do?

_____ .

12. What happened when / tried / return / lottery ticket?

_____ .

13. Who answered / door / second night?

_____ .

14. What / you say?

_____ .

15. What / Mr. Lavigueur say?

_____ .

16. What / do / money?

_____ .

LISTENING AND SPEAKING PRACTICE

SURPRISE!

WITH A GROUP

What do you say when you are really surprised?
Think of as many expressions as you can and write them here.

_____   _____

_____   _____

_____   _____

_____   _____

WITH A PARTNER

William goes to Jean-Guy's house to return the lottery ticket.
He knocks on the door. Practice the conversation.

JEAN-GUY:	Yes?
WILLIAM:	Um, Mr. Lavigueur?
JEAN-GUY:	That's me.
WILLIAM:	Mr. Lavigueur, uh, I'm the man who returned your lottery ticket.
JEAN-GUY:	Uh-huh.
WILLIAM:	Well, tonight, I'm returning your lottery ticket.
JEAN-GUY:	Ticket?
WILLIAM:	And, it's the winning ticket.
JEAN-GUY:	The winning ticket! **I don't believe it! Are you serious!** Come on in. Sit down.
WILLIAM:	So, the ticket's worth $7 650 267.00.
JEAN-GUY:	**You're joking!** Let me see it. Are you sure?
WILLIAM:	It's the winning ticket alright. I checked it in the newspaper five or six times already.
JEAN-GUY:	**This is fantastic! I don't know what to say!** Wait, let me get my cheque book.*

Continue the conversation, and then practice it again using the expressions at the top of the page to express Jean-Guy's surprise.

*Instructor's Manual
Blackboard Dialogue and Supplementary Writing Activities

CHAPTER 11

LIFE ON OTHER PLANETS

Dorothy shows her photos of UFO's.

WITH A GROUP

Discuss these questions:

1. Which planet do we live on?

2. What other planets do you know about?

3. Do you think there is life on other planets? Why or why not?

4. Do you think extra–terrestrials have visited our planet? If yes, ...
   a) What do you think they look like?
   b) Do you think they are more or less intelligent than we are?
   c) How do you think they communicate with each other?
   d) Why would they want to visit us?
   e) How would they get here?

This is a story about Dorothy Izatt, a Vancouver woman, who has seen UFO's (space ships) and has communicated with extra–terrestrials. Write four questions you have about the story.

1. _____ ?

2. _____ ?

3. _____ ?

4. _____ ?

AGREEMENT OR DISAGREEMENT

Here are some ways to express agreement and disagreement.

Strong↑ ↓Weak	**Agreement**	Strong↑ ↓Weak	**Disagreement**
	You're absolutely right!		That's ridiculous!
	I'm with you!		No way!
	I think so too!		Give me a break!
	I agree.		I disagree.
	That's true.		I don't really agree with that.
	Possibly.		I'm not so sure about that.
	Could be.		Well, I don't know about that.

WITH A GROUP

One person reads the numbered statements below and everyone else tells if they agree or disagree and why. Use the expressions above to express agreement or disagreement.

1. The government is not telling us everything they know about UFO's.
2. Some people have seen UFO's.
3. There is life on other planets.
4. There is life on all other planets.
5. Extra–terrestrials have visited the planet Earth.
6. There are extra–terrestrials living on Earth right now.
7. There are some extra–terrestrials in this classroom!
8. UFO's are all different shapes and sizes.
9. UFO's are usually round or spherical.
10. UFO's are usually egg–shaped.
11. UFO's are usually diamond–shaped.
12. Extra–terrestrials can speak English.
13. Extra–terrestrials can speak all languages.
14. Extra–terrestrials can communicate through mental telepathy.
15. Some people can communicate through mental telepathy.
16. Extra–terrestrials don't have any hair.
17. Extra–terrestrials have pointed ears.
18. Extra–terrestrials look like children.
19. Extra–terrestrials are green.
20. Extra–terrestrials can live forever.

IT HAPPENED IN VANCOUVER

FACTS:

■ This province joined Canada in 1871.

■ This is the only province which lies on the Pacific Ocean.

■ Seventy–one percent of the people live in the southwestern part of the province.

■ Fifty percent of the population lives in Greater Vancouver.

■ Vancouver has the second best climate in Canada.

WITH A GROUP

Find Vancouver on your map of Canada. Answer these questions:

1. Which province is Vancouver in? Write it on the map.

    _____

2. Is Vancouver in eastern or western Canada?

    _____

3. What do you know about Vancouver?

    _____

4. Do you think Vancouverites are different from other Canadians? Why or why not?

    _____

VISITORS FROM ABOVE

Dorothy Izatt

VANCOUVER, B.C. — Dorothy Izatt is a Vancouver housewife, mother, grandmother, and

5　great grandmother. She lives in an apartment with her husband and works part-time as a cashier in a large department store. Most

10　people think she is an ordinary person, but she isn't!

On November 9, 1974, Dorothy saw her first UFO. She looked out the window and saw a large, bright

15　object. She said it looked like an enormous diamond shining in the sky.

Later that evening, she went back to the window and saw the

20　UFO again. She wanted to communicate with the space ship so she went to get a flashlight. Every time she moved the flashlight, the UFO moved in the

same way. For three nights in a　25
row, Dorothy communicated with the ship.

Since 1974, Dorothy has seen many UFO's and she has pictures to prove it. Scientists from around　30
the world have looked at the photographs, and they say the photos are real.

Sometimes, the extra-terrestrials visit Dorothy in her Vancouver　35
home. They look human, but they are light beings. Dorothy communicates with them through mental telepathy, but they won't tell her where they are from. Every　40
time she asks, they just look at her and smile!

Dorothy says that the light beings have a message for all of us　45
here on Earth:
"Time is short! Now is the time for the light to grow. It's your job to pass the light to others."

*Instructor's Manual
Original Newspaper Article

DO YOU UNDERSTAND THE STORY?

QUESTIONS AND ANSWERS

WITH A GROUP

Talk about each question and write a group answer.

1. Why do most people think Dorothy is ordinary?

   _____

2. What makes Dorothy different from most people?

   _____

3. When did Dorothy see her first UFO?

   _____

4. How did she communicate with it?

   _____

5. Why did she take pictures of the UFO's?

   _____

6. What do scientists say about the photographs?

   _____

7. How does Dorothy communicate with the extra–terrestrials?

   _____

**8. Why won't they tell Dorothy where they are from?

   _____

**9. Where do you think they are from?

   _____

10. What message do the light beings have for everyone?

   _____

11. What do you think the message means?

   _____

135

DO YOU UNDERSTAND THE STORY?
UNIDENTIFIED FLYING OBJECT

WITH A PARTNER Retell the story.

Retell the story with the class.

WORDS, WORDS, WORDS!

CROSSWORD PUZZLE

WITH A GROUP

Read the clues and write answers from the story in the puzzle.

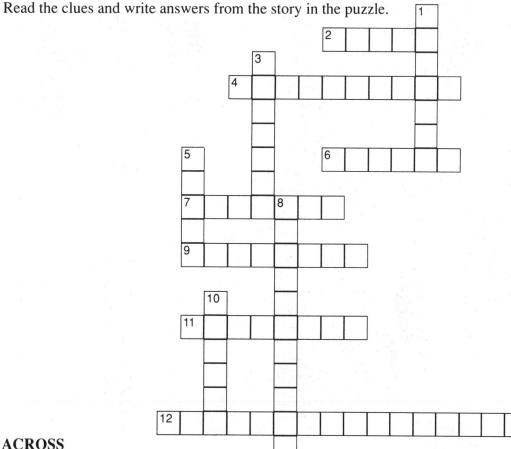

ACROSS

2. We all live on the planet _____ .
4. This store is so big, I can't find the shoe _____ .
6. People are also called human _____ .
7. How many _____ do you see on the table?
9. The space ship was really big. It was _____ .
11. Today is just like any other day. It's an _____ day.
12. A person from another planet is called an _____ _____ .

DOWN

1. Can you turn off the light. It's _____ in my eyes.
3. I'm sorry he's not home right now. Can I take a _____ .
5. She can _____ she is a citizen with her citizenship card.
8. I am learning English so I can _____ with other Canadians.
10. The stars are very _____ tonight.

LANGUAGE PRACTICE

INTERVIEW: You work for the newspaper.

WORK IN GROUPS OF THREE

1. Write questions to ask Dorothy. Put the words in order.
2. Practice the interview. One person is a newspaper reporter; one person is Dorothy; one person checks the answer key.

1. have – you – Do – children

   _____ ?

2. you – Where – do – live

   _____ ?

3. do – with – live – Who(m) – you

   _____ ?

4. work – Where – do – you

   _____ ?

5. first – your – UFO – see – When – did – you

   _____ ?

6. look – it – did – What – like

   _____ ?

7. see – again – Did – it – you

   _____ ?

8. bring – you – What – you – with – did

   _____ ?

LANGUAGE PRACTICE

Change roles.

9. happened – when – moved – flashlight – the – you – What

_____ ?

10 communicate – you – did – How – UFO – with – many – nights – the

_____ ?

11. any – UFO's – Have – you – seen – 1974 – since

_____ ?

12. prove – it – How – can – you

_____ ?

13. extra–terrestrials – ever – talked – Have – you – to

_____ ?

14. What – you – ask – did

_____ ?

15. they – did – How – answer

_____ ?

16. message – extra–terrestrials – us – for – have – the – do – What

_____ ?

PRESENT PERFECT

WITH THE CLASS

1. Write the past participle of each verb.
2. Ask the questions to your classmates. Find someone who answers "yes" to each question. Write their name.

NAME	VERB

1. _____ has _____ (hear) another story about a UFO.

2. _____ has _____ (read) another story about a UFO.

3. _____ has _____ (see) a movie or television program about UFOs or extra–terrestrials.

4. _____ has _____ (see) a UFO.

5. _____ has _____ (speak) to an extra–terrestrial.

6. _____ has _____ (talk) to a Canadian.

7. _____ has _____ (speak) to an American.

8. _____ has _____ (meet) an interesting person.

9. _____ has _____ (go) to an interesting place.

10. _____ has _____ (visit) another city in Canada.

11. _____ has _____ (communicate) through mental telepathy.

12. _____ has _____ (have) a dream about the future.

Ask each person another question.

ANOTHER STORY ABOUT A UFO

Read this newspaper article. If you do not understand a word, try to guess the meaning.

CLOSE ENCOUNTERS IN AUSTRALIA

SYDNEY, AUSTRALIA — Two groups of Australians called police at almost the same time to report a UFO and police say they are taking the reports seriously.

A family of four said an egg–shaped object chased their car while they were driving down the highway. The UFO picked their car off the ground and covered it with ash. Minutes later, fishermen on a tuna boat, fifty kilometres away, said they were buzzed by a UFO and then, they all began to speak in strange voices.

Car driver, Faye Knowles, also told police that her voice and the voices of her three sons had changed during the highway encounter. Trucker, Graham Hawley, who found Mrs. Knowles, said he also saw the UFO. Police didn't believe it at first, but after they saw the car covered in the strange black powder, they didn't know what to think.

Sean, Knowles' 21–year–old son said, "We heard a loud noise on the roof and then it started lifting us. We started to yell but our voices had changed." The mother said, "I didn't know where I was. I reached out of the window and touched the hood of the car. It was soft, warm, and spongy."

Police say they believe the reports because different groups reported the UFO at almost the same time.

Match the new words with their meanings.

close encounter _____	1. soft like a sponge
take something seriously _____	2. unusual, not normal
chase _____	3. scream
ash _____	4. top, front of car
strange _____	5. black powder from burning
encounter _____	6. run after
yell _____	7. believe something
hood _____	8. call in
spongy _____	9. meeting
report _____	10. meeting with extra–terrestrials

Reread the story and write ten questions to ask your partner.

CHAPTER 12

WHAT'S THE STORY?

WITH A GROUP

Look at this newspaper photo and fill in the missing words in the story below.
Then, check the answer key.

During his two–_____ ¹ world tour, Rick travelled through four _____ ² :

Europe, Asia, _____ ³ and _____ _____ ⁴ . He completed the 40

073 km journey to raise money for _____ ⁵ people around the world.

What other information do you know about this important Canadian news story?

RICK WHEELS AROUND THE WORLD!

WITH THE INSTRUCTOR Answer questions about the pictures and tell the story together.

Retell the story with a partner.

* Instructor's Manual
Simplified Text and Picture Card Masters

Why do people think of Rick Hansen as a Canadian hero?

May 23

RICK HANSEN: A CANADIAN HERO

CANADA — It was the summer of 1973 and a young Rick Hansen was riding home in the back of a pick-up truck. Suddenly, the truck went out of control and turned over. Rick landed on the ground and broke his back. The doctor told him he was paralysed from the waist down.

This was a terrible shock, but only a year later, Rick had a great idea. He thought about going around the world in a wheelchair. He wanted to raise money for other people with physical disabilities.

To prepare himself for this incredible journey, Rick competed as a wheelchair athlete and won championships in volleyball and basketball. He also got a degree in Physical Education at the University of British Columbia.

On March 21, 1985, Rick started his world tour. He left from Oakridge Shopping Mall in Vancouver and had problems from the start. Only 300 invited guests came to see him off. Most of the shoppers didn't pay attention. As the team drove out of the parking lot, they went under a low overpass and the roof rack fell off their truck.

During the two year tour, Rick wheeled over five mountain ranges and through four continents. He experienced all kinds of weather conditions, including snow storms heat waves and a flood. He was robbed four times, used eighty pairs of gloves and had one hundred flat tires!

The most difficult challenge was in China when he climbed the Great Wall. It was a very steep incline, and it took all of his strength to push the chair upward — but he didn't give up.

And it was lucky he didn't because Rick did complete his 40 073 journey around the world. He arrived back at Oakridge Mall on May 22, 1987 — and this time there were 10 000 people there to greet him! Rick is a Canadian hero. He raised $23 000 000.00 for spinal-cord research, and continues working to help the physically challenged, in Canada and around the world.

*Instructor's Manual
Original Newspaper Article

DO YOU UNDERSTAND THE STORY?

PROBLEMS AND ACCOMPLISHMENTS

WITH A PARTNER

Reread the story and list Rick's problems and accomplishments.

PROBLEMS

1. _____
2. _____
3. _____
4. _____
5. _____
6. _____

ACCOMPLISHMENTS

1. _____
2. _____
3. _____
4. _____
5. _____
6. _____

CLASS DISCUSSION

1. What does Rick's story tell us about the human spirit?
2. Aside from the money, how did Rick's journey help people with disabilities?

EXTRA

Make a list of the problems and accomplishments in your life and talk about them with a partner.

DO YOU UNDERSTAND THE STORY?

TABLE OF EVENTS

WITH A PARTNER

Do you know what Rick did in 1986? Check the "Table of Events" below for the answer. Then, complete it with information from the story.

TABLE OF EVENTS

1973	
1974	
1975–84	
1985	
1986	Rick asked his physiotherapist to marry him!
1987	
1988	
1990	Rick and Amanda had a baby!

Complete a "Table of Events" for your own life. Write the year and tell what happened. Then talk about the events with your partner.

MY TABLE OF EVENTS

19 _____	
19 _____	
19 _____	
19 _____	
19 _____	
19 _____	
19 _____	

WORDS, WORDS, WORDS!

CROSSWORD PUZZLE

WITH A GROUP Read the clues and write words from the story in the puzzle.

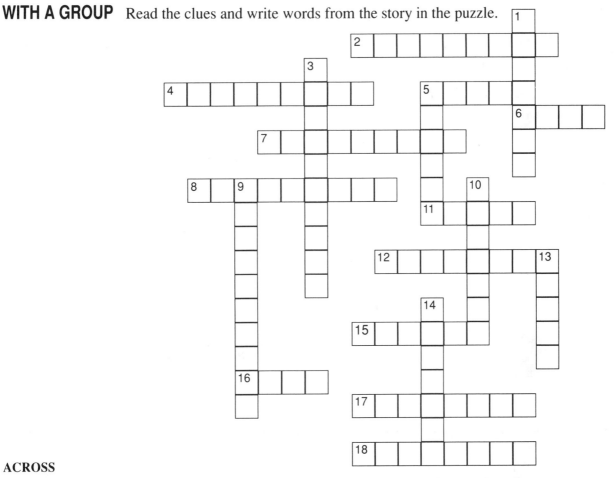

ACROSS

2. Students should pay _____ to the teacher.
4. Learning English is a _____ .
5. Can you _____ someone in another language?
6. He puts his school books on his bicycle_____ .
7. If you can't move a part of your body, it's _____ .
8. The rent is $600.00 _____ hydro and parking.
11. Sometimes, it is a _____ when you move to a new country.
12. An _____ is a road that goes over another road.
15. When you graduate from university, you get a _____ .
16. Rick's world _____ lasted two years.

17. A person in a wheelchair is a _____ person.
18. Scientists do _____ to find cures for disease.

DOWN

1. She lost _____ of the car during the accident.
3. Rick Hansen is an _____ man.
5. They invited 150 _____ to their wedding.
9. Australia and North America are _____ .
10. Athletes _____ for gold medals at the Olympic Games.
13. It is difficult to climb a _____ hill.
14. Many people do not _____ dinner at home; they go to restaurants.

149

LANGUAGE PRACTICE

INTERVIEW: You work for the newspaper.

WITH A PARTNER

Make up questions to ask Rick about his life. Use the pictures to help you. Then, practice the interview with your partner. One person is the newspaper reporter and the other is Rick Hansen.

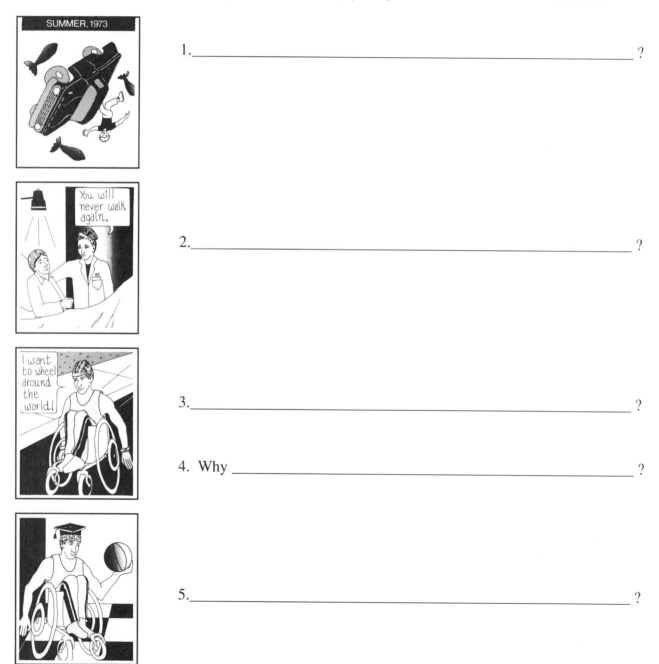

1. _____ ?

2. _____ ?

3. _____ ?

4. Why _____ ?

5. _____ ?

LANGUAGE PRACTICE

Change roles.

6._____?

7._____?

8._____?

9._____?

10._____?

11._____?

12._____?

READING PRACTICE

STUDENT COMPOSITION

Read this composition written by Miyuki Takaesu, a Japanese student studying English in Vancouver. Answer these questions:

1. What is the difference between the disabled people in Canada and those in Japan?

   _____

2. What does Miyuki want to do for disabled people in Japan?

   _____

SAME AS US

    I often see people in wheelchairs around Vancouver. I wonder why there are so many people here with disabilities. Then, I remember seeing disabled people in Japan as well. But in Japan, people with disabilities hide in their homes. Maybe this is because there aren't enough special washrooms, elevators, or ramps for them. Maybe there are too many people on the streets and there just isn't enough room for them. Maybe they think they are different from us and feel uncomfortable.   5

    In Canada, people with disabilities are very active. They run, swim, and shop, go to movies, and take the skytrain! I see them at baseball games and at the bank. I see them and think that they are not really different from us. I think about the physically challenged in Japan. We should think about their lives more.   10

    In the future, I would like to be an architect. My dream is to build houses and equipment for people with disabilities in Japan. I want them to feel comfortable like disabled people in Canada, and love their lives.

EXPRESS YOURSELF

WITH THE CLASS

Talk about these questions and then answer one of them in a short paragraph.

1. Aside from being paralysed and in a wheelchair, what other kinds of disabilities can people have?
2. Do you know anyone with a disability? Tell about their life.
3. What modern inventions have helped people with disabilities?
4. Can you think of any other ways to help people with disabilities?
5. Why do some people mistreat disabled people?
6. How are people with disabilities treated in your country?
7. How do you feel about people with disabilities?

Appendix

COORDINATING READING SKILLS WITH A GENERAL LANGUAGE PROGRAM

CHAPTER	LEVEL	GRAMMAR	FUNCTION	DISCUSSION	CANADIANA
1: Wheat Farmer Asks Big Question	Mid-beginner	Will Past tense Question words	Inviting	Marriage and wedding customs	Mapping - Facts Crop farming in Canada
2: Debbie's Dog	Mid-high beginner	Can Commands Past tense When	Complimenting Giving advice*	Pets Discrimination	Mapping - Facts
3. Roop Catches Falling Child	High-beginner	Two-word verbs Past tense Past continuous tense Adverbs When	Thanking*	Becoming a Canadian citizen	Mapping - Facts Application for citizenship Interview with a judge
4: Lovers United	High beginner	Present continuous tense Past tense Past continuous tense Will When	Promising* Leave taking*	World travel Hometown Marriage	Immigrating to Canada
5: Mr. Fix-it	High beginner	Present habitual vs. past tense When	Requesting*	Opening your own business	Mapping - Facts
6: Sharon Wood Climbs Mount Everest	High beginner	Past tense Comparatives Superlatives When Enough	Making inquiries*	What is your dream?	Mapping - Facts The Canadian flag

* See instructor's notes for specific chapter.

COORDINATING READING SKILLS WITH A GENERAL LANGUAGE PROGRAM

CHAPTER	LEVEL	GRAMMAR	FUNCTION	DISCUSSION	CANADIANA
7: Atima Gets the Job	High beginner	Past tense Present habitual tense When After	Asking for and reporting information*	Jobs Job interviews	Mapping - Facts The Inuit
8: Canadian Learns Chinese	High beginner	Habitual vs. past tense Will Superlatives	Expressing likes and dislikes	Free time activities Learning a language	Mapping - Facts Canada has two official languages
9: Loretta Lobster Flies Home!	High beginner	Past tense Have to	Requesting*	Fishing and cooking	Mapping - Facts Canadian industry
10. Honest Ticket-Finder Gets Reward	High beginner — pre-intermediate	Past tense Gerunds and infinitives	Expressing surprise	Lotteries What would you do if you won?	Mapping - Facts
11. Unidentified Flying Object	Pre-intermediate	Past tense Present perfect tense Since	Expressing agreement and disagreement	Life on other planets	Mapping - Facts
12: Rick Hansen Wheels Around the World	Low-intermediate	Past tense During As When	Sympathizing* Congratulating*	People with disabilities	A Canadian hero

* See instructor's notes for specific chapter.

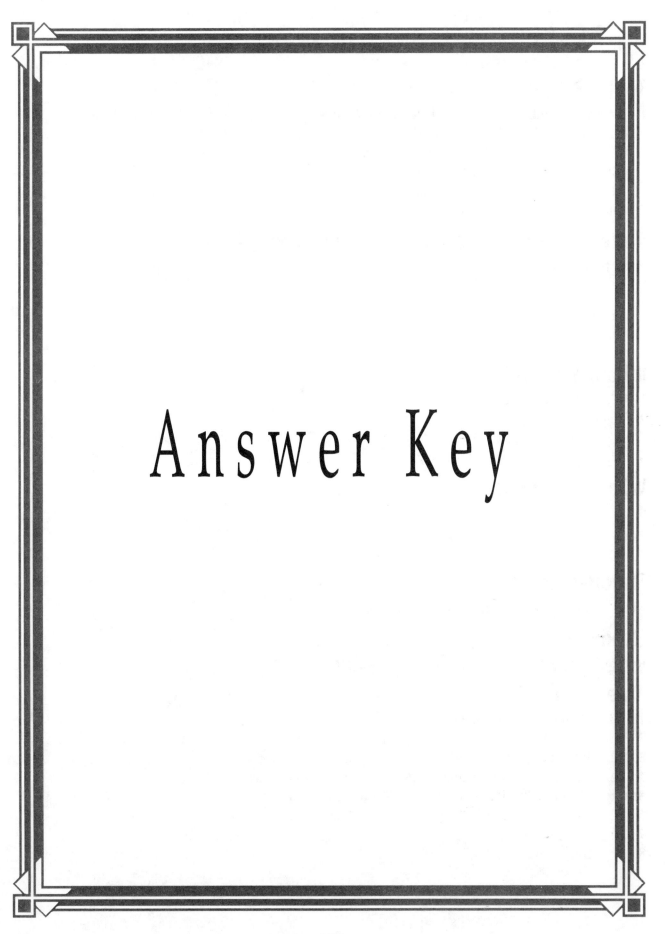

Answer Key

INTRODUCTION

To the Student

1. British Columbia, Alberta, Saskatchewan, Manitoba, Ontario, Quebec, Newfoundland, New Brunswick, Nova Scotia, Prince Edward Island
2. The Yukon Territory, The Northwest Territories
3. The Atlantic Ocean is east of Canada.
4. The Pacific Ocean is west of Canada.
5. Ottawa is the capital of Canada.

Write the Names of Canada's Provinces and Territories

Refer to the "Quiz Key" in the instructor's manual.

CHAPTER 1

It Happened in Milestone

1. It's in Saskatchewan.
2. Regina is the capital.
3. It's in western Canada.
4. They grow wheat and other grains.

What Happens Next?

3,7,4
6,1,5
2,9,8

Reading for Answers

Refer to the "Quiz Key" in the instructor's manual.

Headlines

Refer to the "Quiz Key" in the instructor's manual.

True or False?

1. T: He thought of the idea.
2. F: Chuck lives in Milestone; Cecile lives in Regina.
3. F: It took him four hours and forty–five minutes.
4. F: Chuck cut it alone because he wanted to surprise Cecile.
5. F: He wrote, "Will you marry me Cecile? Love Chuck."
6. F: Chuck is the only farmer who proposed this way.
7. T: He rented the plane.
8. T: She answered "Yes."

Word Families

1. worker
2. marriage
3. smiled
4. proposal

---

1. worker, works
2. marriage, marry
3. smiled, smile
4. proposed, proposal

Interview Chuck: You work for the newspaper.

1. What	2. Where	3. How old	4. Who	5. Where
6. What kind	7. How much	8. What	9. How	10. How long
11. Why	12. How long	13. Why	14. What	

CHAPTER 2

It Happened in Vancouver

1. It's in British Columbia.
2. It's in western Canada.
3. Answers will be different.
4. There isn't much snow in Vancouver.

Questions and Answers

1. She is in a wheelchair because she can't move her arms or legs very much. She is a disabled person.
2. She got a dog to help her with the many things she cannot do.
3. He went to dog training school.
4. They paid $7875.00.
5. Answers will be different.
6. Answers will be different.

The Eighty Commands

Refer to the "Quiz Key" in the instructor's manual.

Prefixes

a) disabled
b) nonprofit
c) dislikes
d) disabilities
e) nonreturnable
f) nonprofit
g) nonfat
h) displeased
i) disinterested
j) nonstop

1. Nonfat   2. nonreturnable   3. dislikes   4. displeased

5. disabilities   6. disinterested   7. nonstop   8. nonprofit

Discrimination

8, 1, 9, 2, 3, 7, 5, 6, 4

Questions and Answers

1. Debbie is thirty–seven years old.
2. She is blind.
3. She has a guide dog.
4. He helps her to find her way around.
5. She went to a restaurant.
6. He brought a coffee.
7. Alex, the restaurant owner, came in.
8. He told them to get out.
9. She said that was discrimination and against the law.
10. No, the dog did not disturb anyone.
11. Alex said, "I make the laws...and you can take your laws with you."
12. She felt angry.
13. She took Alex to court.
14. The judge made Alex pay $300.00.
15. Alex said, "I am very sorry. Debbie can come into my restaurant anytime she wants."
16. Answers will be different.

CHAPTER 3

It Happened in Toronto

1. It's in Ontario.
2. It's Toronto.
3. Ottawa, the capital of Canada, is in this province.
4. Answers will be different.

What's the Story?

1. highrise apartment building
2. Roop Sandhu
3. balcony
4. catch

What Happens Next?

6,2,4,
8,1,9
3,5,7

Reading For Answers

Refer to the"Quiz Key" in the instructor's manual.

Headlines

Refer to the "Quiz Key" in the instructor's manual.

Interview: You work for the newspaper.

1. Where does the Minhas family live?
   They live on the sixth floor of a highrise apartment building just outside Toronto.
2. Where did the mother go?
   She went to work.
3. What did the father and son do?
   They watched TV.
4. What happened after a while?
   They fell asleep.
5. Why did Eric wake up?
   He heard some children playing outside.
6. What did he push onto the balcony?
   He pushed a chair onto the balcony.
7. How did he get to the edge of the balcony?
   He climbed up the chair.
8. What happened then?
   He fell over the edge.
9. How long did he hold on?
   He held on for two minutes.
10. What did he scream?
    He screamed, "Daddy, Daddy!"
11. Where were you at the time?
    I was fixing my car.
12. What did you do?
    I ran one hundred metres, and jumped over a 1.2 metre fence.
13. Why did you catch the boy?
    I didn't want him to be hurt.
14. How did you feel?
    I was happy that Eric was alive.

Opposites

1. highrise	2. asleep	3. playing	4. outside
5. pushed	6. scream	7. young	8. quickly
9. threw	10. emigrated		

You Don't Need a Dictionary!

1. climbed	2. accidentally	3. edge	4. hurt
5. scream	6. fixing	7. tools	8. metres
9. fence	10. save	11. quickly	12. knocked

Becoming a Canadian Citizen

Refer to the "Quiz Key" in the instructor's manual.

CHAPTER 4

Why?

Your answers may be different.

1. The tour only lasted three weeks.
2. The government wasn't delivering the mail.
3. She got a divorce from her first husband.
4. He was married to other women.
5. At that time, it was very difficult to emigrate from the Soviet Union.

You Don't Need a Dictionary!

Refer to the "Quiz Key" in the instructor's manual.

Correct the Mistakes

Refer to the "Quiz Key" in the instructor's manual.

CHAPTER 5

It Happened in Edmonton

1. It's in Alberta.
2. It's in western Canada.
3. Answers will be different.

Interview: You work for the newspaper.

1. What <u>is</u> Noel's job?
   He <u>is</u> a handyman
2. Where <u>is</u> he from?
   He <u>is</u> from <u>Edmonton</u>.
3. What <u>did</u> he have when he started his business?
   He <u>had</u> a truck and some tools.
4. What jobs can he <u>do</u>?
   He <u>can</u> take out garbage and mow lawns.
5. What other jobs <u>can</u> he do?
   He <u>can</u> do plumbing and plastering.
6. What else <u>can</u> he do?
   He <u>can</u> build sundecks and fix electrical wiring.
7. What <u>did</u> he do when he started his business?
   He <u>put</u> an ad in the <u>newspaper</u>.
8. What <u>did</u> it say?
   It <u>said</u>, "Attention: Widows, divorcees, single ladies! Get a <u>husband</u> without the <u>problems</u> ..."
9. What happened after the ad <u>was</u> in the paper?
   He <u>got</u> a lot of crank calls from <u>women</u>.
10. What <u>did</u> he do then?

He changed his <u>ad</u>.

11. Who(m) <u>does</u> he work for now?
    He <u>works</u> for men, <u>women, seniors, and handicapped people</u>.
12. How much <u>does</u> he charge per visit?
    He <u>charges</u> $50.00 a visit.
13. Where <u>does</u> he plan to open companies?
    He <u>plans</u> to open companies across <u>Canada</u> and around the <u>world</u>.
14. What <u>is</u> the name of the company?
    It <u>is</u> called "Mr. Fix–It."

What's the Big Idea

1. b   2. c   3. a   4. c

Why?

Your answers may be different.
1. He needed the money.
2. He needs a place to put his tools and he needs a vehicle to drive to people's houses.
3. Because he thought he would get lots of business.
4. He didn't want any more crank calls.
5. Because it's good for business.
6. Because he wants to become a rich businessman.

Compound Words

Refer to the "Quiz Key" in the instructor's manual.

CHAPTER 6

What's the Story?

1. Nova   2. Columbia   3. woman   4. metre

It Happened in the Rockies

1) The Rockies are a group of mountains in western Canada.
2) They run along the border of British Columbia and Alberta.
3) The name "Rockies" comes from the word "rocks."
4) Answers will be different.

Reading For Answers

Refer to the "Quiz Key" in the instructor's manual.

Headlines

Refer to the "Quiz Key" in the instructor's manual.

Sharon: Child, Teenager, and Adult

Child – para. <u>1</u>   Teenager – para. <u>2</u>   Adult – para. <u>3</u>
a, d, h, l   e, f, g, j   b, c, i, k

You Don't need a Dictionary!

1) j   2) d, h   3) f, b   4) e   5) c   6) g, i, a

Interview: You work for the newspaper.

1. How many children are there in your family?
   There are four children in my family.
2. Where did you go with your father?
   I went on hikes in the woods.
3. Did your father like to climb hills and rocks?
   No, he liked to walk around them.
4. What did you do when you were fifteen?
   I quit school.
5. Was your father angry?
   No, he wasn't.
6. What did you do when you were seventeen?
   I left home to take a rock-climbing course
7. What did Laurie Skreslet say about your climbing?
   He said I was a better climber than he was.
8. Who was Laurie Skreslet?
   He was the first Canadian to climb Mount Everest.
9. What was your dream?
   I wanted to climb Mount Everest.
10. When did you begin to climb Mount Everest?
    I began in March, 1986.
11. Who did you climb with?
    I climbed with a team of Canadians.
12. Why did only two people go to the summit?
    Because there was only a little oxygen.
13. What did you put on the summit?
    I put the Canadian flag on the summit.
14. Why was your climb important?
    I was the first Canadian woman to climb Mount Everest.

CHAPTER 7

It Happened Near Spence Bay

1. It's in the Northwest Territories.
2. It's very cold in winter, but in the summer, temperatures are moderate. There is a time in the winter when there is no sunlight.
3. They are called the Inuit. They speak Inuktitut.

What Happens Next?

Refer to the "Quiz Key" in the instructor's manual.

What Does "It" Mean?

Paragraph 2

them: the children

it: landing on the ice

his: Atima's

Paragraph 3

this: he didn't have a good job and didn't make much money

Paragraph 4

it: his decision

Why?

Your answers may be different.

1. The school was far away.
2. The plane that took the children to school couldn't land on the ice anymore, so Atima had no way of getting to school.
3. He didn't have a very good education.
4. He wanted to get a better education.
5. He needed a better job to support his family, and he needed more schooling to get a better job.
6. He could speak two languages.

Word Families

Refer to the "Quiz Key" in the instructor's manual.

The Inuit

1. igloo or snowhouse
2. fur
3. rifle

Filling Out an Application

1. What is your family name?
2. What is your given name?
3. What is your middle name?
4. What is your address?
5. What city? What city do you live in?
6. What province? What province do you live in?
7. What country? What country do you live in?
8. What is your postal code?
9. What is your residence phone number?
10. Do you have a business phone number?
11. What is your social insurance number?
12. What is your date of birth?
13. What was the last grade you completed?
14. Do you have any other training?
15. What languages do you speak?

16. What languages do you write?
17. What was your last job? What was your position? What was the name of the company?
18. What was the address?
19. Do you have any references? What are their names and addresses?
20. What is today's date?
21. Can you sign here please?

CHAPTER 8

What Do You Like Doing in Your Free Time?

1. cycling
2. swimming
3. playing soccer
4. reading
5. sleeping
6. dancing
7. travelling
8. cooking
9. going to restaurants
10. ironing
11. playing/listening to music
12. talking on the phone
13. watching TV

It Happened in Ottawa

1) It is in Ontario.
2) It is the capital of Canada.
3) They speak English and French.
4) Answers will be different.

What's the Story?

1) He is holding two certificates.
2) I see the Chinese or Mandarin language.
3) I think he learned to speak Chinese.
4) Answers will be different.

Reading For Answers

Refer to the "Quiz Key" in the instructor's manual.

Why?

1) He liked a challenge.
2) Because all of the other children would have one or two Chinese parents to practice with.
3) It was difficult to learn to write the language.
4) He was learning about the Chinese culture.
5) Answers will be different.
6) Answers will be different.

Crossword Puzzle

Across	Down
1. worried	2. official
4. hobby	3. challenge
7. cultures	5. graduated
9. character	6. Mandarin
10. difficult	7. crafts
	8. symbol

Canada Has Two Official Languages

Refer to the "Quiz Key" in the instructor's manual.

CHAPTER 9

It Happened in Lockeport

1. It's in Nova Scotia.
2. The Atlantic Ocean surrounds this province.
3. They are called the Atlantic Provinces.
4. Many people work in the fishing industry

What's the Big Idea?

2) a   3) b   4) b   5) b   6) b   7) c

Words That Go Together

lobster trapping
Atlantic waters
lobster expert
set her free
wooden traps
huge lobster
perfect condition
lobster wholesaler
free of charge
swim away

1. huge lobster	2. lobster expert	3. swim away	4. perfect condition
5. lobster wholesaler	6. Lobster trapping	7. Atlantic waters	8. wooden traps
9. free of charge	10. set her free		

The Yellow Pages

1. 641–2111	2. 276–7310	3. 278–2131	4. 682–1411
5. 689–9166	6. 682–1411		

Canadian Industry

Refer to the "Quiz Key" in the instructor's manual.

CHAPTER 10

What's the Question?

What would you do if you won a million dollars? or
What would you do if you won the lottery?

It Happened in Montreal

1. It's in Quebec.
2. Answers will be different.
3. Answers will be different.
4. They speak English and French.

What Does "It" Mean?

him—Jean–Guy
you—Jean–Guy
your—Jean–Guy's
it—the ticket
you—William
I—Jean–Guy
his—Jean–Guy's
They—the family

Reading For Answers

Refer to the "Quiz Key" in the instructor's manual.

Mixed Feelings

Refer to the "Quiz Key" in the instructor's manual.

Word Families

Refer to the "Quiz Key" in the instructor's manual.

Interview: You work for the newspaper.

1. Where do you live?
   I live in a small room in Montreal.
2. Do you have a job?
   No, I'm unemployed.
3. How much money do you have in the bank?
   I have fifty–six cents in the bank.
4. What did you find on the street?
   I found a wallet on the street.
5. What was inside?
   There was some identification, six lottery tickets and eighteen dollars.
6. What did you do with the wallet?
   I put it in the mailbox.

7. What did you do with the tickets?

    I kept them.

8. Why did you keep them?

    I thought I might win $10.00 or something.

9. Where did you check the lottery numbers?

    I checked them in the newspaper.

10. How did you feel?

    I was so surprised, I thought I was going to have a heart attack.

11. What did you decide to do?

    I decided to return the ticket.

12. What happened when you tried to return the ticket?

    Yves, told me to go away.

13. Who answered the door the second night?

    Jean–Guy answered the door.

14. What did you say?

    I said, "You are a millionaire Mr. Lavigueur. This is your ticket."

15. What did Mr. Lavigueur say?

    He said, "You are an honest man. I'm giving you a $1.2 million reward."

16. What are you going to do with the money?

    I'm planning to go skiing in Vancouver.

CHAPTER 11

It Happened in Vancouver

1. It's in British Columbia.
2. It's in western Canada.
3. Answers will be different.
4. Answers will be different.

Questions and Answers

1. Because she lives in an apartment with her husband, works part–time, and has a nice family. She seems to have an ordinary life.
2. She has seen UFO's.
3. She saw it on November 9, 1974.
4. She used a flashlight to communicate with it.
5. She took pictures to prove she saw the UFO's.

    She wanted other people to believe her.
6. Scientists say the photographs are real.
7. She communicates with them through mental telepathy.
8. Answers will be different.
9. Answers will be different.
10. They say, "Time is short! Now is the time for the light to grow. It's your job to pass the light to others."
11. Answers will be different.

Crossword Puzzle

Across

2. earth
4. department
6. beings
7. objects
9. enormous
11. ordinary
12. extra–terrestrial

Down

1. shining
3. message
5. prove
8. communicate
10. bright

Interview: You work for the newspaper.

1. Do you have children?
   Yes, I have children, grandchildren and great–grandchildren.
2. Where do you live?
   I live in an apartment in Vancouver.
3. Who(m) do you live with?
   I live with my husband.
4. Where do you work?
   I work in a large department store.
5. When did you see your first UFO?
   I saw it on November 9, 1974.
6. What did it look like?
   It looked like an enormous diamond shining in the sky.
7. Did you see it again?
   Yes, I saw it later that evening.
8. What did you bring with you?
   I brought a flashlight.
9. What happened when you moved the flashlight?
   The space ship moved in the same way.
10. How many nights did you communicate with the UFO?
    I communicated with it for three nights in a row.
11. Have you seen any UFO's since 1974?
    Yes, I have seen many UFO's.
12. How can you prove it?
    I took photographs and scientists say they are real.
13. Have you ever talked to extra–terrestrials?
    No, but, I have communicated with them using mental telepathy.
14. What did you ask?
    I asked many questions including, "Where are you from?"
15. How did they answer?
    They smiled.
16. What message do extra–terrestrials have for us?
    They say, "Time is short! Now is the time for the light to grow. It's your job to pass the light to others."

Present Perfect
Refer to the "Quiz Key" in the instructor's manual.

Another Story About a UFO
10, 7, 6, 5, 2, 9, 3, 4, 1, 8

CHAPTER 12

What the Story?
1. year
2. continents
3. Australia
4. North America
5. disabled

Problems and Accomplishments
Refer to the "Quiz Key" in the instructor's manual.

Table of Events
1973   Rick was in an accident and broke his back.
1974   He decided to wheel around the world to help people with disabilities.
75–84   He competed as a world–class athlete and won championships in volleyball and basketball. He also got a degree at the University of British Columbia.
1985   He started his world tour.
1986   He asked his physiotherapist to marry him.
1987   He completed his world tour.
1988   He continues to help the physically challenged in Canada and around the world.
1990   Rick and Amanda had a baby!

Crossword Puzzle

Across
2. attention
4. challenge
5. greet
6. rack
7. paralysed
8. including
11. shock
12. overpass
15. degree
16. tour
17. disabled
18. research

Down
1. control
3. incredible
5. guests
9. continents
10. compete
13. steep
14. prepare

Student Composition
1. Disabled people are more active in Canada.
2. She wants to build houses and other equipment for them.

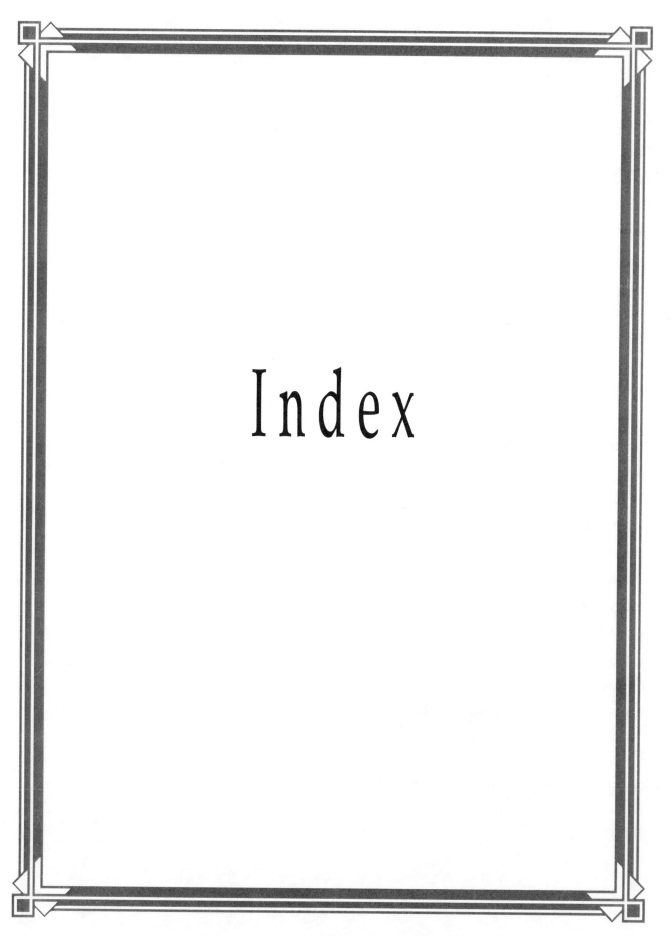

Index

CANADIANA INDEX

LANGUAGE INDEX